ISSUES IN HOLOCAUST EDUCATION

For Sam, Jake and Harry
and
Danny and Vanessa

Issues in Holocaust Education

GEOFFREY SHORT
University of Hertfordshire, UK

CAROLE ANN REED
*Formerly, Director of the Holocaust Education and
Memorial Centre, Toronto*

ASHGATE

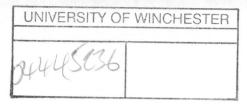
Published by
Ashgate Publishing Limited
Gower House
Croft Road
Aldershot
Hants GU11 3HR
England

Ashgate Publishing Company
Suite 420
101 Cherry Street
Burlington, VT 05401-4405
USA

Ashgate website: http://www.ashgate.com

British Library Cataloguing in Publication Data
Short, Geoffrey
    Issues in Holocaust education
    1. Holocaust, Jewish (1939-1945) - Study and teaching
    (Secondary) 2. Holocaust, Jewish (1939-1945) - Study and
    teaching (Elementary)
    I. Title II. Reed, Carole Ann
    940.5'318'071

Library of Congress Cataloging-in-Publication Data
Short, Geoffrey.
    Issues in Holocaust education / Geoffrey Short, Carole Ann Reed.
        p. cm.
    Includes bibliographical references and indexes.
    ISBN 0-7546-4210-0
    1. Holocaust, Jewish (1939-1945)--Study and teaching. I. Reed, Carole Ann,
    1946- II. Title.

    D804.33.S57 2004
    940.53'18'071--dc22

                                      2004000034
ISBN (Hbk) 0 7546 4210 0
ISBN (Pbk) 0 7546 4211 9

Printed and bound in Great Britain by MPG Books Ltd, Bodmin, Cornwall

Contents

Preface

In this book we set out to explore the nature of Holocaust education in schools. We do so, in part, by examining a range of theoretical issues including the need for such education, the factors that influence its evolution and the reasons for the antiracist movement's indifference to the Holocaust and its place in the curriculum. The book's empirical core sheds light on the attitudes and practices of teachers and on the prospects of drawing on the Holocaust to promote responsible citizenship. We acknowledge that our contribution is a personal one, for the theoretical, historical and instructional issues we have chosen to address reflect our experiences and priorities as Holocaust educators in the United Kingdom and Canada. As we deal in the main with developments in these two countries, our contribution is partial as well as personal, for we would not wish to claim that the situation in either country is representative of what has happened elsewhere. Indeed, such a possibility is remote given the diverse nature of national representations of the Holocaust (Huyssen, 1994). Our hope is that academics in other parts of the world will engage with the issues we raise, replicate and extend our research and, in the process, forge a better understanding of the limitations and possibilities of teaching the Holocaust to young children and adolescents.

Whatever the book's shortcomings, it is undoubtedly timely, for the curriculum in many schools in the United Kingdom and Canada, and in various other countries, has responded to a level of interest in the Holocaust that is not only unprecedented but shows no signs of abating. Certainly, in the United Kingdom it would seem that over the past ten years or so the Holocaust and its aftermath, in one form or another, have rarely been out of the news. Both the print and broadcast media, for example, covered the arrest and trial of the war criminals Maurice Papon and Anthony Sawoniuk and reported on the acquittal, in Israel, of the suspected death camp guard John Demjanjuk. In addition, they helped bring to public notice a number of academic controversies, notably those involving Daniel Goldhagen's (1996) claims about the part played by 'ordinary Germans' during the Nazi era; William Rubinstein's (1997) defence of the Allies' decision not to bomb Auschwitz and John Cornwell's (1999) condemnation of the role of Pius XII. Moreover, there was a point in the mid-1990s when the news agenda gave prominence to attempts to restore expropriated Jewish property to its rightful owners, the best known case involving an investigation into the 'dormant accounts' of Holocaust victims in Swiss banks. A few years later considerable publicity was generated by David Irving's libel trial (and his unsuccessful appeal) and also by Norman Finkelstein's (2000) blistering polemic against 'the Holocaust industry.' However, it is not just the reporting of current affairs that has prevented the Holocaust receding from consciousness, for popular culture and especially the cinema have also had a significant impact. Films such as *Schindler's List*, *Life is Beautiful* and *The Pianist* stand out, for all three were not only highly successful in terms of box office receipts, Oscar nominations and awards; they were also much discussed, and in the case of *Life is Beautiful*, much debated. More recently, Costa-Gavras's film *Amen*, which accuses the Vatican of turning a blind eye to the destruction of European Jewry, caused an outcry in certain quarters and, as we write, *Rosenstrasse* looks set to do likewise. Directed by Margareta von Trotta, it challenges received wisdom on the effectiveness of the demonstration by a group of 'Aryan' women in Berlin in February 1943 on behalf of their imprisoned Jewish husbands.

Partly in response to these and other developments (such as acts of contrition by church leaders) the Holocaust, for many people, has come to symbolise the ultimate expression of evil. It is thus not surprising that while its teaching at secondary school level may be mandated in only a handful of countries, its value in relation to citizenship education has increasingly been recognised. Nowhere more so, perhaps, than at the International Forum on the Holocaust in Stockholm where, in January 2000, many of the world's Prime Ministers and Heads of State gathered to express their determination to heed the lessons of Nazi racial policy. The Forum was convened as a result of a commitment given by the Task Force for International Co-operation on Holocaust Education, Remembrance and Research set up at the behest of the Swedish Prime Minister, Göran Persson, in May 1998. Persson chaired the conference and helped draft the agreed declaration that urged 'governments to ensure that future generations can understand the causes of the Holocaust and reflect upon its consequences.'

Further evidence that teaching the subject is being taken seriously at the highest levels can be seen in the work of the Council of Europe. Founded in 1949 to protect and promote human rights, the organisation has taken steps over recent years to raise the profile of Holocaust education among its 41 member states and especially among those emerging from Communist rule. The commitment of the Council to this project was evident in the speech delivered by its Secretary General, Walter Schwimmer, at the Stockholm conference. He said:

> I consider teaching about the Holocaust, its roots and consequences, a crucial obligation. It constitutes a necessary part of every young person's education, whatever their national and cultural background. We must be vigilant ... because there are those who claim that 'we have already heard enough about this.' We never will hear enough about it.
>
> (Schwimmer, 2000)

Support for this point of view is to be found not only in the growing tendency in many parts of the world to include the Holocaust in school curricula (see Wyman, 1996a), but in the number of countries that have established Holocaust memorial days, for such occasions invariably have education as one of their primary purposes. However, the assumption that teaching about this cataclysmic event is necessarily 'a good thing' and can only advantage those who learn about it is not universally shared. On the contrary, a body of academic opinion is clearly sceptical of the claim. We consider the arguments of two well-known detractors, Peter Novick (1999) and Lionel Kochan (1989) in the opening chapter which assesses the case for and against teaching the Holocaust in schools. In quite a few countries the case has clearly been won, although victory was a long time in coming. In Chapter 2 we explore the factors responsible for the absence of Holocaust education for so many years in the United Kingdom and Canada and for its gradual emergence in both countries in the 1970s.

While some may dispute the claim that there are lessons to be learnt from the Holocaust, the contribution the subject can make to deepening students' understanding of racism is self-evident. The potential scope of this contribution is suggested by one of the recommendations in the final report of the British Government's advisory group on citizenship (Department for Education and Employment [DfEE], 1998). It states that at the end of Key Stage 3 of the National Curriculum, pupils (aged 14) should:

> understand the rights and responsibilities underpinning a democratic society, with particular reference to the European Convention on Human Rights; be aware of issues surrounding rights such as freedom of speech and freedom from arbitrary arrest; know about the Universal Declaration of Human Rights and why it was developed; *also understand the meaning of terms such as prejudice, xenophobia, discrimination, (and) pluralism.*
>
> (DfEE, 1998:49. Original emphasis)

As we will make clear, the Holocaust can assist teachers to combat racism in other ways too. It is therefore perplexing and disturbing to discover that, for the most part, the antiracist movement historically has eschewed any interest in how the subject is taught in schools. Indeed, apart from our own work, we know of only one study arguing that the Holocaust should play an integral role in antiracist education (see Wells and Wingate, 1985). In Chapter 3 we attempt to resolve this paradoxical situation.

While advocating that the Holocaust be included in the secondary school curriculum, we acknowledge that teaching the subject is potentially fraught with problems. In the first instance, questions arise in relation to appropriate content although some issues are manifestly less contentious than others. No one, for example, could condone teaching the Holocaust in a way that leads students to believe, or allows them to conclude, that the Germans are uniquely or inherently vulnerable to racism in general and anti-Semitism in particular. Other issues though, such as whether teachers ought to make reference to Holocaust denial, are less clear-cut. There are also pedagogical challenges that have to be faced, such as meeting the needs of less able students and ensuring that all possible steps are taken, within reason, to avoid trauma. In addition, teachers have to consider whether to permit the expression of racist points of view and, if so, how, if at all, they should respond. Finally, there are ethical questions to be addressed such as whether it is ever legitimate for teachers to make use of resources knowing that they may cause pain to some of their pupils. Chapter 4 deals at length with a number of these and related issues and also highlights aspects of school organisation relevant to teaching the Holocaust. The need to pay especially close attention to curricular content is suggested by a survey carried out several years ago in Germany where Holocaust education is mandatory in all sixteen states. It found that nearly a third of 14- to 18-year-olds had never heard of the Auschwitz death camp and more than half had no knowledge of the *Kristallnacht* pogrom (*The Times*, July 2, 1998). In so far as these findings are reliable, the ignorance they reveal reflects one of a multiplicity of ways in which Holocaust education can fail. In order to gain insight into how the subject is taught in the United Kingdom and Canada, history staff in secondary schools in the London area and in metropolitan Toronto were interviewed about their attitude towards teaching the Holocaust, the problems they encounter and the ways they endeavour to overcome them. The research also attempted to assess the value or otherwise of a number of textbooks currently in use in both countries. Chapter 5 summarises the results.

In a sense, Chapter 6 returns to the contentious issue of the lessons the Holocaust can teach, for it comprises an evaluation of what students learn about citizenship (and specifically about racism) as a result of engaging with the Holocaust as history. It reports and elaborates upon the findings of a small-scale ethnographic study carried out with a group of 14- and 15-year-olds in south-east England.

Chapters 7 and 8 are concerned with the resources available to teachers of the Holocaust and, in particular, with the usefulness of museums and commercially produced curricula. In respect of the latter, the distinguished historian, Lucy Dawidowicz (1992) published a scathing critique some years ago in which she condemned many of the 25 curricula she examined in the United States on the grounds of their misleading content and damaging pedagogy. She raised fears relating to historical accuracy and methods of teaching (explicitly questioning the benefits of role play) and warned of the dangers of political indoctrination. In order to assess the current validity of her strictures, we critically appraise two Holocaust curricula in widespread use; one in the United Kingdom, the other in North America. The curricula were selected partly on account of their contrasting priorities, as the chapter also aims to illustrate the range of concerns of Holocaust educators.

The expansion in the number of Holocaust museums throughout the world bears further testimony to the subject's growing popularity. The last two decades have witnessed the establishment of such museums in many countries, some of which are geographically distant from the sites of destruction in eastern Europe. In the United States, the largest of the twenty or so museums was opened in Washington DC in 1993 and attracts in excess of two million visitors annually. In Japan, a country with which Jews, historically, have had almost no connection, a museum was founded in Fukuyama in 1995 dedicated to the million or more Jewish children murdered by the Nazis. Its success led to the building of a second centre in Tokyo in 1998. The following year a Holocaust museum opened in Cape Town, South Africa and, in our own countries, we note the existence of four museums in Canada (in Toronto, Montreal, Vancouver and Saint John) and two in the United Kingdom (in London and Nottingham) with the possibility of a third in Manchester, where a project that had made some headway has now been shelved because of financial difficulties. The Nottingham museum, incidentally, was the first of its kind to open in western Europe (other than those at camp sites). But despite the exponential increase in their number, it should not be assumed that Holocaust museums are an unqualified blessing for, in common with Holocaust curricula, they have the potential to lead astray as well as to edify (see, for example, Cole, 1999; Short, 2000a). In light of this caution, we look closely in Chapter 8 at the contribution the museums in Nottingham and Toronto are likely to make to students' knowledge and understanding of the Holocaust.

The final issue we address is whether the Holocaust can usefully be taught in the primary or elementary school and if it can be taught at this level, whether it should be. Unfortunately, the discussion is largely theoretical, for there is very little in the way of empirical evidence that can shed light on the matter. There are certainly no convincing data on the impact of Holocaust education on young children's thinking or on their emotions. The general dearth of research in this field of education is a topic discussed at greater length in the Endnote.

A Note on Terminology

We are aware that we have not, so far, offered a definition of the Holocaust or considered the appropriateness of the word when writing about the Nazi era. The issue of definition has proved the more contentious, as was evident in the acrimonious debate that occurred in the United States in the late 1970s between Simon Wiesenthal and President Carter on the one hand and Elie Wiesel and Yehuda Bauer on the other. The sharp exchanges took place during the early stages of planning the National Holocaust Museum in Washington DC and related to whether 'the Holocaust' should refer only to the six million or so Jews murdered by the Nazis or should include, in addition, the millions of other victims of Nazi brutality. Wiesel and Bauer wanted the narrower definition and it is our choice too, though not for any of the reasons that (according to Novick, *op. cit.*) were advanced at the time. We have not, for example, been influenced by Wiesel's insistence 'on the temporal as well as the conceptual priority of Jewish victimhood'

(Novick, *ibid.*, 218). Nor are we persuaded by arguments such as those put forward by Guenter Lewy (1999). He maintains that:

> the term "Holocaust" stands for the attempted physical destruction of an entire people, pursued with relentless determination, and, in its most lethal phase, carried out with the mass-production methods of a modern factory. Only the Jews were caught up in this kind of murderous enterprise.
>
> (Lewy, 1999:399)

Our view is not just that the attitudes and policies of the Nazis towards their various victim groups were different, but that this crucial fact may be obscured, especially for young adolescents, if the same word is used to describe the fate of every group that suffered under the Nazis. That said, we feel strongly that teaching the Holocaust will descend into farce if it is presented in such a way as to give the impression that the Jews were the Nazis' only victims or that they alone were deemed unworthy of life. We would therefore urge teachers, when dealing with the Holocaust, to make more than a token acknowledgement of the fate of the Roma and Sinti and the Slavs, and those who were persecuted on grounds other than ethnicity such as Jehovah's Witnesses, homosexuals, political opponents and Germans with disabilities. We do not, however, advocate this inclusive approach merely for reasons of historical truth, for we are also concerned that in coming to terms with the Holocaust, students should learn something about the nature of racism and, not least, that those with a pathological need to hate rarely have a single target in their sights (Adorno *et al.*, 1950).

Despite gaining widespread currency in the 1960s, the use of the word 'Holocaust' has always been problematic. This is partly due to the way it has been applied indiscriminately to almost any large-scale human suffering, no matter how little that suffering has in common with 'the war against the Jews.' One well-regarded dictionary in the United Kingdom actually defines the word as 'great destruction or loss of life, or the source of such destruction,' but the literal meaning of 'Holocaust' as 'a whole burnt offering' has also caused difficulty. The manifestly sacrificial connotation of the phrase and its suggestion of a theological explanation for the genocide proved offensive to some commentators who consequently sought an alternative nomenclature. Many orthodox Jews employ the term 'the third churban,' or destruction, the previous two referring to the razing of the First and Second Temples. Far more people, however, now speak of the Shoah, a Hebrew word taken from the book of Isaiah (10:3) meaning 'ruin,' 'destruction' or 'desolation.' It has increasingly found favour with writers, particularly in France where, at one time, 'catastrophe' had been the preferred term. But 'Holocaust' remains the epithet most often invoked to refer to the attempted annihilation of the Jews of Europe and it is for this reason that we have chosen to use it.

Acknowledgements

We owe a debt of gratitude to a number of people who have helped bring this book to fruition. In particular, we wish to thank Dr. Susan Tegel, formerly of the University of Hertfordshire, who commented at length on an early draft and improved it immeasurably. Prior to leaving the university, to concentrate on her own writing, Susan often revealed her extensive knowledge of the Holocaust in informal discussions with Geoffrey Short; a trafficking in ideas from which he benefited considerably. We are grateful too to Dr. Stephen Smith, Director of the Beth Shalom Holocaust Centre in Nottinghamshire. With characteristic kindness, he agreed to check that we had not misrepresented either the Centre or the leading role that he and his family played in establishing it. Elsewhere in the book we address issues informed by the empirical work that we have carried out over the past ten years. We would like to record our appreciation of the many teachers and pupils in British and Canadian schools who consented to take part in the research and, in the process, furthered our understanding of what Holocaust education entails.

Special mention must also be made of a small group of people who pioneered Holocaust education in Ontario during the mid and late 1970s and who have continued to the present day to make seminal contributions to teaching about the Holocaust and human rights. This group includes Frank Bialystok who willingly shared his erudition, his contacts and even his personal library with Carole Ann Reed when she was a graduate student just beginning to enter the field of Holocaust studies; Myra Novogrodsky, an inspired teacher who allowed Carole access to her classroom and offered her encouragement and friendship and Harold Lass, another generous and committed teacher who has become a much valued colleague of Carole's on a number of projects. We owe a great deal to them all as well as to Margaret Wells who, along with Frank and Harold, read a draft of the book when it was near to completion. Their insightful and constructive suggestions are warmly acknowledged. In addition to these friends and colleagues, Carole wishes to thank her husband Daniel and daughter Vanessa for their unfailing support.

Finally, we are obliged to the publishers Taylor and Francis, Frank Cass, The Johns Hopkins University Press and the Christian Education Movement who have allowed us to draw on the following articles:

Abella, I. and Bialystok, F. Canada, in: Wyman, D. S. (1996) (Ed.) *The World Reacts to the Holocaust*, Baltimore, The Johns Hopkins University Press.

Cesarani, D. Great Britain, in: Wyman, D. S. (1996) (Ed.) *The World Reacts to the Holocaust*, Baltimore, The Johns Hopkins University Press.

Short, G. Teaching the Holocaust: Some reflections on a problematic area, *British Journal of Religious Education*, 14, 1, pp. 28-34.

Short, G. Holocaust education in Ontario high schools: An antidote to racism? *Cambridge Journal of Education*, 30, 2, pp. 291-306.

Short, G. The Holocaust in the National Curriculum: A survey of teachers' attitudes and practices, *Journal of Holocaust Education*, 4, pp. 167-188.

Short, G. Holocaust Education and Citizenship: A view from the United Kingdom, in: Leicester, M., Modgil, C. and Modgil, S. (Eds.) *Education, Culture and Values: Vol. VI* (London, Falmer Press).

Chapter 1

Why Teach about the Holocaust?

The Promotion of Understanding

It is our contention that if the Holocaust is taught well the case for its inclusion in the school curriculum is unassailable. Whether or not one goes as far as Daniel Goldhagen (1996:4) in viewing the attempted annihilation of European Jewry as 'the most shocking event of the (twentieth) century,' it was, indisputably, one of the watershed events of that century and some may consider this, in itself, sufficient justification for teaching it. The Holocaust, however, is more than just a major historical landmark, for its unprecedented character enables us to construe the past in a different light and also helps shape our perception of seminal developments in our own time. Certainly, aspects of world history since 1945 and, most obviously, developments in the Middle East, cannot fully be comprehended without some awareness of the fate of the Jews in Nazi-occupied Europe. The Holocaust exemplifies a body of knowledge that 'constantly throws light on, widens and deepens (our) view of countless other things' (Peters, 1966:159) and, as such, an awareness of its significance can be seen as a defining characteristic of an educated person. But nothing that has been said thus far makes the case for granting space in the curriculum to the Holocaust, rather than to some other historical event that appreciably expands our understanding. Schools, of necessity, have to be selective in their curricular content, and to press the claims of the Holocaust we should note the view of some philosophers of education that becoming educated also involves an understanding of persons or, 'knowledge of our own and other minds' (Hirst and Peters, 1970:63). For this purpose, study of the Holocaust appears ideally suited as there can be no more potent illustration of the depths of human depravity or the resilience of the human spirit. It is difficult to envisage a medium more conducive to learning about the psychology of prejudice, obedience, conformity and altruism; nor one more likely to stimulate discussion of the antecedent variables that predispose some of us to acquire these attributes and others to reject them. Learning about the Holocaust also shows the importance of taking into account a host of socio-historical factors as well as psychological ones if we are fully to understand the darker side of human behaviour.

The Role of the Holocaust in Developing Political Literacy

The most compelling reason for studying the Holocaust is to help secure the future against further violations of human rights whether based on ethnicity, religion, gender, sexual orientation or disability. The eighteenth-century British statesman and political theorist, Edmund Burke, famously remarked that 'the only thing necessary for the triumph of evil is for good men to do nothing.' Arguably, the Holocaust illustrates the truth of this contention as powerfully as any episode in human history, but one of the preconditions of individuals taking action against evil is that they recognise the evil for what it is in good time. In the words of the renowned writer and Auschwitz survivor, Primo Levi (1987:396), 'We cannot understand (the Holocaust) but we can and must understand from where it springs and we must be on our guard. If understanding is impossible, knowing is imperative, because what happened could happen again.' It is the need to foster such knowledge and understanding in the hope of preventing a repetition that constitutes much of the *raison d'être* for teaching the Holocaust in schools. Indeed, at a time when many societies, culturally more diverse than ever before, are threatened by a rising tide of nationalism and xenophobia, a study of the Holocaust would seem to deserve the highest priority. Not only can the subject contribute to students' understanding of racism, by illustrating the nature of critical concepts such as scapegoating, stereotyping and nationalism; it can also make plain the socio-political, economic, historical and psychological conditions under which racism is likely to flourish. Moreover, the Holocaust offers an opportunity to demonstrate an important dimension of the prejudiced frame of mind that came to light in the well-known, if controversial, American study, *The Authoritarian Personality* published in 1950. The authors, Theodor Adorno and his colleagues, claimed that highly prejudiced individuals rarely have an antipathy towards a specific group, such as Jews, but are antagonistic towards all outgroups and 'aliens.' The eminent social psychologist, Gordon Allport (1954), in his seminal text, *The Nature of Prejudice*, strongly concurred:

> One of the facts of which we are most certain is that people who reject one out-group will tend to reject other out-groups. If a person is anti-Jewish he is likely to be anti-Catholic, anti-Negro, anti-any out-group.
>
> (Allport, 1954:68)

The range of 'undesirables' targeted by the Nazis clearly testifies to the truth of this contention and teachers should deepen their students' understanding of the racist mindset by discussing Nazi policy towards the Slavs, the Roma and Sinti, homosexuals and the disabled. They might also allude to the Nazi attitude towards Muslims for the same reason. [Alfred Rosenberg (1934:665), the Nazis' key racial theorist, warned in his book *The Myth of the Twentieth Century* that the white peoples of Europe should be on their guard 'against the united hatreds of coloured races and mongrels led in the fanatical spirit of Mohammed.']

In the context of racism, learning about the Holocaust has other benefits too, not the least of which is that it highlights the dangers of allowing the growth of an incipient xenophobia to go unchecked. Students acquainted with the Holocaust can hardly fail to appreciate that racism is not a phenomenon restricted by its nature to name-calling in the playground or discrimination in the labour and housing markets. On the contrary, they are forced to recognise it as a virulent toxin that can involve unimaginable brutality and lead to the cold-blooded and systematic slaughter of millions. In a multi-ethnic society, such knowledge is an essential component of responsible citizenship.

While the Holocaust may be useful in helping students learn about various facets of racism, it is an ideal medium for enabling them to understand and combat anti-Semitism. In the course of their socialisation, students of secondary school age may well acquire the same sort of misconceptions about Jews that were prevalent in Germany and elsewhere during the Nazi era (see Chapter 4). Studying the Holocaust and the years leading up to it provides teachers with an opportunity to focus upon and expose the ill-founded basis of these beliefs. Moreover, a study of the Holocaust can not only shed light on the nature of anti-Semitism and of racism in general, but has the advantage of doing so 'naturally.' By this we mean that the subject is acknowledged by all except those on the lunatic fringe to be an integral part of the Second World War and, as such, is not likely to be regarded by students as an irrelevance inserted into the curriculum for reasons of political correctness. In contrast, activities that fall under the rubric of conventional antiracist education may well be seen in this way and, as a result, fail to make headway in dislodging racist beliefs. [We elaborate on this point in Chapter 3.]

In relation to political literacy more broadly defined, a study of the Holocaust and the socio-political developments that gave rise to it, may prompt students to consider the measures that liberal democracies need to take in order to safeguard their fundamental freedoms. They may debate, for example, whether such societies should extend the principle of free speech to members of political parties who are unwilling to extend it to others. They may reflect on whether the interests of human rights are best served by the authorities failing to take action against suspected war criminals simply because the passage of time has diminished the chances of a successful prosecution. And they may also think about the responsibilities of the individual when confronted by evil, for one of the potential benefits of studying the Holocaust is that it can demonstrate, by focusing on the activities of rescuers, that people are not necessarily reduced to the role of impotent bystanders in the face of oppressive dictatorships; individuals can be seen to make a difference. Indeed, by focusing on the heroism of ordinary men and women who risked their lives, and often the lives of their families to protect Jews, students can observe that people much like themselves can make a difference. At the same time, by learning of the failure of the mass of the population in Nazi-occupied Europe to hide and care for Jews, the reluctance of the churches to speak out and the refusal of many countries to take substantial numbers of refugees, students may come to appreciate more fully than they otherwise might, the dangers inherent in turning a blind eye to evil. Finally, the Holocaust provides students with an opportunity to reflect critically on aspects of their own culture (and, above all, on its religious and literary traditions) that depict ethnic minorities in an unfavourable light and to reflect further on the implications of such a depiction (Julius, 2000). In sum, learning about the Holocaust can constitute an educational experience that allows the democratic majority to protect itself against the consequences of racist discourse, demagoguery and propaganda.

Holocaust Denial

An additional reason for studying the Holocaust is the need to combat denial. We know that much of the physical evidence of the camps was deliberately destroyed by the Nazis in the latter stages of the war and as a result, their ideological heirs have felt free to maintain that all talk of death camps is a fiction invented by Jews for political and financial gain. The roots of Holocaust denial can be traced back to Paul Rassinier's *Le Passage de la Ligne* in 1948 (cited in Lipstadt, 1993) and more or less the same deception has been peddled periodically ever since. Scurrilous publications such as *The Rumour of Auschwitz* by Robert Faurisson (1979) and *The Hoax of the Twentieth Century* by Arthur Butz (1976) either dispute the existence of death camps or cast doubt on their capacity to carry out murder on the scale that has been claimed. The authors are all neo-Nazi sympathisers who have sought to rid themselves of the electoral liability of the Holocaust. According to James Dalrymple (1992), these and other revisionist 'historians':

> share one common theme and one common problem. The theme is anti-Semitism and the problem is the Holocaust. The clear evidence that upwards of 6 million Jews were slaughtered by the Nazis stands like a monolithic barrier to (their) ambitions.
>
> (Dalrymple, 1992:207)

For many years it was possible to dismiss the deniers as 'a small group of political extremists and radical-fringe pseudo-historians ... whose arguments (lay) far beyond the accepted pale of scholarly discourse' (Lipstadt, 1992:66). But in recent years their *modus operandi* has changed and they are now attempting to convince:

> the world that they are engaged in a serious historical enterprise. Their books and journals have been given an academic format and they have worked hard to find ways to insinuate themselves into the arena of serious historical debate and deliberation.
>
> (Lipstadt, *ibid.*, 67)

Not everyone, however, agrees that Holocaust denial needs to be taken seriously. In a recently acclaimed book that has attracted a great deal of publicity on both sides of the Atlantic, Peter Novick (*op. cit.*) writes as follows:

> The argument for raising Holocaust consciousness that has been advanced with the greatest urgency is, by any sober evaluation, the most absurd: the alleged necessity of responding to the tiny band of cranks, kooks and misfits who deny that the Holocaust took place.
>
> (Novick, *op.cit.*, 270)

Novick's dismissive attitude towards the threat posed by deniers stems from what he sees as their disturbed psychological state. He refers to them as 'screwballs' and 'fruitcakes' in addition to 'cranks, kooks and misfits' and seems convinced that due to their mental affliction they can safely be ignored. In a similar vein, Finkelstein (*op.cit.*, 68) argues that 'there is no evidence that Holocaust deniers exert any more influence in the United States than the flat-earth society does.' Novick cites a 1994 opinion poll finding in the United States to justify his complacency, for the poll showed that only around one per cent of the respondents doubted the Holocaust's existence. But he conveniently overlooks evidence from outside the United States which arguably paints a much more disturbing picture. In Sweden, for example, a survey carried out in 1996 and 1997 of nearly eight thousand students in sixty towns revealed that 'a third of ... 12- to 18-year-olds do not believe the Nazis' extermination of the Jews ever occurred ...' (de Laine, 1997). It was this finding that prompted Swedish Prime Minister, Göran Perrson, to initiate moves that led to the setting up of the international task force on Holocaust education referred to in the Preface. 'Israeli authorities ... claim similar attitudes (to those found in Sweden) have come to light in Britain, Canada, Germany and France' (Leigh, 1997) and while it does not necessarily follow that high levels of scepticism reflect the influence of Holocaust deniers (Bruchfeld, 2000), the possibility ought not to be discounted. Nor does it follow that psychiatric disturbance offers the only way to account for the failure of deniers to make much headway in the United States. Indeed, we believe, contrary to Novick, that a more convincing explanation for their lack of success is to be found in the high level of Holocaust consciousness in the country. We thus have no hesitation in arguing that Holocaust education should be expanded, and its quality improved, as a bulwark against those who would deny or trivialise the heinous crimes of the Third Reich. While we recognise that the inclusion of the Holocaust in the curriculum is not, in itself, an adequate means of countering the sophistry of the deniers, we have no doubt that its absence from the curriculum will make it easier for them to influence the gullible.

It would be a mistake to associate Holocaust denial only with neo-Nazis, for in recent years the phenomenon has spread widely throughout the Arab world (Fisk, 1996; Matar, 2001) and has played a major role in the ideology of some fundamentalist Muslim groups such as Hizb-ut-Tahrir that actively recruit in the

West. Aware that the Holocaust is often invoked to reinforce the moral justification for modern-day Israel, - 'the certificate of its political legitimacy' to use Bauman's (1989) metaphor - these rabidly anti-Zionist groups have a vested interest in asserting that the Holocaust is a myth 'invented by the Israelis to justify their seizure of Palestinian Arab land' (Fisk, *ibid.*). In so far as Islamic communities throughout the world sympathise with the Palestinian cause, studying the Holocaust (and its aftermath) in an informed and dispassionate manner may help some young Muslims to repudiate those aspects of fundamentalist propaganda that espouse Holocaust denial in order to discredit the Jewish State.

The Limitations of Holocaust Education

As is widely known, the American poet and philosopher, George Santayana (1905) wrote that those who cannot remember the past are condemned to repeat it. Keeping alive the memory of the Holocaust may well be a *sine qua non* of avoiding a recurrence, but Santayana was wrong to emphasise memory rather than understanding and naive to imply that all who learn about the Holocaust will necessarily come to revile it and all it represented. If handled intelligently and with sensitivity, an engagement with the subject may help *some* students to understand and abhor racism in general and anti-Semitism in particular, but it is unlikely to have this effect on all students, for as Gordon Allport (*op. cit.*) pointed out nearly fifty years ago, the racial attitudes of certain individuals are impervious to rational persuasion. He observed that in some people, 'realism is low; the individual neither knows nor cares what the facts are concerning minority groups ... The functional significance of these attitudes lies deep, and nothing short of an upheaval in the character structure will change them' (Allport, 1954:505). However, he was equally insistent:

> that the ethnic attitudes of many individuals lack internal integration. They are shifting and amorphous, and for the most part are linked to the immediate situation. The person himself may be said to be ambivalent - or, more accurately, multivalent, for, lacking a firm attitude structure, he bends with every pressure. It is with this group that pro-tolerance appeals may be effective. ... *This type is susceptible to education.*
>
> (*ibid.*, 505-506. Emphasis added)

The aim of Holocaust education, is thus not to eradicate anti-Semitism and every other manifestation of racism, for as Allport makes clear, there will always be some individuals with a pathological need to hate. But they must never be allowed to influence, let alone dominate, public opinion. The function of Holocaust education is rather to inoculate the generality of the population against racist and anti-Semitic propaganda and thereby restrict its appeal to a disaffected and politically insignificant rump.

Dissenting Voices

Although the Holocaust is taught in schools in a number of countries, and sometimes as part of a statutory curriculum (Wyman, 1996a), it should not be assumed that this development has been universally welcomed by academics otherwise sympathetic to the teaching of Jewish history. In the United Kingdom the best-known critic of Holocaust education in schools is Lionel Kochan, an historian who urged the British Government, when it was planning the National Curriculum, to omit the Holocaust from the history syllabus on the grounds that 'disseminating a knowledge of Nazi barbarism (is) fraught with danger' (Kochan, 1989:25). His argument, in part, echoes Hegel's (1818) assertion that 'what experience and history teach is ... that peoples and governments have never learned anything from history.' In Kochan's own words, 'knowledge of past brutality and violence has never prevented their repetition.' He asks: 'Have all the scholarly investigations into the causes of wars ever prevented a recurrence? We hear a great deal about the supposed "lessons" of the Holocaust (but) the precedent of the "lessons" of war offers no encouragement at all' (*ibid.*). Kochan's main argument, however, concerns the impact of the Holocaust on Jewish children's sense of their ethnic identity. He quotes the former Chief Rabbi of the Commonwealth, Lord Jacobovits, who warned against 'nurturing and breeding a Holocaust mentality of morose despondency among our people, especially our youth.' In the same vein Kochan wonders:

> Who would be a Jew if suffering and persecution were the dominating themes of our history? ... Let Jewish history be taught by all means but ... what masochism is it that promotes (the Holocaust) above all other (subjects)? What is wrong with the Golden Age of Spanish Jewry, or of Polish or German Jewry? ...
>
> (*ibid.*)

In addition to tempting young Jews to 'doubt (their) allegiance,' Kochan fears that teaching the Holocaust will reinforce a perception among the public-at-large of the Jew as 'predestined victim of persecution.' Most seriously of all, he maintains that such teaching will make a repetition of the Holocaust more likely.

> If the Holocaust does have a lesson it is this: not that the knowledge of its horrors will deter any future perpetrator, but that any such perpetrator will learn of a precedent that has been set; that a threshold has been crossed which will serve as a source of encouragement.
>
> (*ibid.*)

It should be noted that Kochan does not object to the Holocaust being studied. He just wishes to stress that 'there is a world of difference between scholarly research and teaching to the immature and unsophisticated.' (It should further be noted that although he makes his comments in relation to the teaching of history, he must, perforce, be equally opposed to teaching the subject through other subjects such as English or religious education; for it would be absurd to object to its inclusion on the grounds he has listed in just one area of the curriculum).

Peter Novick (*op. cit.*) also questions the alleged 'lessons of the Holocaust.' His scepticism is partly grounded in its extreme nature, for he maintains that the event is so far removed from everyday life as to have little to teach us about the way people ordinarily behave. Its exceptional character certainly does not allow us to learn any lessons about victims, perpetrators or bystanders. In addition, Novick criticises what he believes is frequently regarded as 'the principal lesson of the Holocaust,' namely, its ability to sensitise us to man's inhumanity to man. The argument here is that in making the Holocaust 'the benchmark of oppression and atrocity (it trivialises) crimes of lesser magnitude' (*ibid.*, 14). The example he cites is the American debate on the Bosnian conflict, focusing on whether it was 'truly holocaustal or merely genocidal.' After referring to this debate as 'truly disgusting' (an assessment with which we wholeheartedly agree) Novick proceeds to talk about other lessons of the Holocaust which he describes as 'empty' and 'not very useful.' These include 'the revelation that science and technology are not necessarily benevolent' and the claim that the Holocaust disabuses us of Enlightenment illusions about the perfectibility of man.

We will respond to Novick's criticisms shortly. First, we want to pick up on some of the points raised by Kochan who appears to believe that learning about the Holocaust in schools can only have deleterious consequences for students whatever their ethnic or religious background and regardless of how well the subject may be taught.

Responding to the Critics

Kochan sounds a useful note of caution when considering the impact of learning about the Holocaust on the way that the public-at-large perceives Jews and on how Jewish children may come to perceive themselves. As Ronnie Landau (1992:13) points out, 'all too often students of the Holocaust confront no other picture of the Jew except one of unrelieved torment and victimisation. This can create an obsessive and utterly unbalanced view of the entire Jewish role in history and, for that matter, of all Jews.' Yet the preferred way to obviate this admitted disadvantage of Holocaust education is surely not to omit the subject from the curriculum, as Kochan advocates, but rather to teach Jewish history more honestly; and that means stressing the triumphs of the Jewish people as well as the tragedies.

It may well be the case that only in Jewish schools can sufficient time be set aside to cover in depth the glorious episodes in the Jewish past alluded to by Kochan, but students in all schools should at least be made aware that the history of the Jewish people is far from synonymous with persecution and suffering. Teachers should know and inform their pupils that 'the lachrymose conception of Jewish history' (Baron, 1952) is a misleading one. But even if schools were to accede to Kochan's request and exclude the Holocaust from the curriculum, that would hardly guarantee its invisibility. The subject is constantly in the news; it is addressed in newspaper articles, discussed on television and on the radio and is easily accessible via the Internet. References to it are present in the literature that adolescents read, and from time to time the subject is featured in film and on stage. Stopping students from making contact with the Holocaust is thus not an option. The issue is not whether, but *how*, they are to be introduced to it. Would Kochan be happy if, instead of learning about the Holocaust in school, students familiarised themselves with it from films like *Life is Beautiful*? - a fable whose depiction of the Holocaust was described by the historian David Cesarani (1999) as 'misleading and pernicious.' If schools do not accept responsibility for promoting an informed understanding of the Holocaust, any number of undesirable agencies may step in to fill the vacuum. The danger in such an eventuality is that students' 'knowledge' of the attempted annihilation of European Jewry would amount to little more than a farrago of half-truths and untruths.

Kochan's least convincing objection to schools teaching the Holocaust is that potential perpetrators will learn of a precedent having been established and derive encouragement from such knowledge. He writes in such a way as to suggest that psychopaths who may be contemplating mass murder have only the Holocaust as their guide and inspiration, when, in truth, if they need any such inspiration, they are able to choose from an assortment of more or less 'successful' genocides that have scarred the twentieth century. Kochan also writes as though unaware that Hitler was prompted to give vent to his apocalyptic fantasies by his belief that the international community had forgotten about an earlier case of genocide. In a speech delivered to high-ranking army officers on the eve of Germany's invasion of Poland, Hitler is alleged to have said:

> Ghengis Khan had millions of women and men killed by his own will and with a gay heart. History sees in him only a great state builder ... and I have sent to the east ... my 'Death's Head Units', with the order to kill without mercy men, women and children of Polish race or language. Only in such a way will we win the 'Lebensraum' that we need. Who, after all, talks nowadays of the extermination of the Armenians?
>
> (Fein, 1979:4)

Turning next to consider Kochan's claim that the Holocaust has no lessons worth learning, we deal first with the analogy he draws between the Holocaust and the history of warfare. He asserts that scholarly research into the causes of war, as well as the numerous memorials bearing the inscription 'never again', have failed to prevent the recurrence of war and the truth of this claim can hardly be denied. However, while the analogy may be valid, the argument is specious, for it overlooks the crucial distinction between a historical event providing lessons and those lessons being learned. It is incontrovertibly the case that there have been many instances of genocide since 1945, but it is a *non sequitur* to argue, from this fact alone, that the Holocaust has nothing to teach us. One could just as plausibly argue that the genocides have occurred because there has been so *little* in the way of Holocaust education for much of the past fifty years. In the light of this speculation, it may be no coincidence that Nato's intervention in Kosovo came at a time when Holocaust education in many European states and in North America was being taken more seriously than ever before. Indeed, both President Clinton and Prime Minister Blair justified the bombing of Serbia with reference to the Holocaust. *The Times* reported that:

> In an impassioned speech to local government workers, Mr. Clinton compared the Serb assault on ethnic Albanians in Kosovo to Nazi atrocities and asked how many lives would have been saved "if people had listened to Churchill and stood up to Hitler earlier."
>
> (*The Times*, March 24, 1999)

Tony Blair was even more explicit. He drew powerful parallels between the ethnic cleansing perpetrated by Milosevic and 'what Hitler ... did to the Jews 50 years ago' (*Jewish Chronicle*, May 21, 1999).

In our view, the Holocaust and the events leading up to it do contain useful lessons. They relate, for example, to the dangers of unrestricted free speech and to the demand that influential organisations, such as the Church, speak out against evil. We recognise, though, that some lessons have not been learnt. Arguably, the most pressing, as far as schools are concerned, is the need to educate against racism and to do so with the full and active support of the government. In the United Kingdom, however, both Margaret Thatcher and John Major when Prime Minister, publicly denounced antiracist education at their annual party conferences (in 1987 and 1992 respectively). Similarly, in Canada, one of the first casualties of the retrenchment of the mid-1990s in the province of Ontario was the anti-racism secretariat (Harney, 1996).

We believe that Novick's criticisms are also flawed. It will be recalled that his sceptical attitude towards learning anything of value from the Holocaust is based partly on the latter's extreme nature and thus its inability to speak to the situation that most of us encounter in our day-to-day lives. In his view, 'There are ... more important lessons about how easily we become victimisers to be drawn from the behaviour of normal Americans in normal times than from the behaviour of the SS in wartime' (*op.cit.*, 13). He has in mind the ground-breaking experiments carried out by social psychologist Stanley Milgram (1974) in the 1960s and 1970s which showed 'how willingly the most ordinary people, in the most ordinary circumstances, would comply with barbaric instructions' (*ibid.*, 245). Leaving aside the question of just how ordinary it is for participants in an experiment on learning to be asked and paid by a professor to administer high-voltage electric shocks to complete strangers (Baumrind, 1964), Novick appears to have misunderstood the purpose of Holocaust education. At issue is not only the lessons to be learnt from observing the way people behave in extreme conditions, but the lessons to be learnt from studying how a relatively normal society can be transformed into a highly abnormal one infused with a lethal racist ideology. As Landau (*op. cit.*, 5) puts it: 'How on earth was it possible for such a supposedly civilised society, which had given us Goethe, Beethoven and Brahms, to produce such barbarity, albeit of a largely dispassionate and coolly executed kind?'

Novick is also critical of the centrality accorded to the Holocaust in American life on the grounds that it desensitises us to other tragedies.

> The principal lesson of the Holocaust, it is frequently said, (is) that it sensitises us to oppression and atrocity. In principle it might, and I don't doubt that sometimes it does. But making it the benchmark of oppression and atrocity works in precisely the opposite direction, trivialising crimes of lesser magnitude.
>
> (Novick, *op.cit.*, 14)

Our response to this criticism is to state bluntly that making the Holocaust 'the benchmark of oppression and atrocity' is wholly at variance with our understanding of good Holocaust education precisely because it is likely to numb, rather than sharpen, that sensitivity to injustice which we seek. Singling out the Holocaust in this way is the very antithesis of sensitivity to other people's suffering. The problem, as Novick (*ibid.*, 15) acknowledges, 'is connected to the axiom of the uniqueness of the Holocaust and its corollary, that comparing anything to the Holocaust is illegitimate ...' We do not propose to enter into this debate, for while the uniqueness or otherwise of the Holocaust may be an issue of considerable interest to historians and philosophers (see, for example, Katz, 1994 and Brecher, 1999), it has only limited significance for educationalists. Its value to the teacher is restricted to disabusing students of the belief that all victims of genocide have suffered for the same reason, a point we consider more fully in Chapter 4.

Novick's final criticism causes us fewer problems. We agree that many of the so-called lessons of the Holocaust are 'empty' and 'not very useful,' but these are not the sort of lessons we see as justifying its inclusion in the curriculum.

Chapter 2

The Development of Holocaust Education in the United Kingdom and Canada

In so far as schools reflect and reproduce the dominant culture, the seriousness with which the Holocaust is treated in the curriculum will mirror its salience in the wider society. For decades after the Second World War there was little public awareness of the Holocaust in either the United Kingdom or in Canada and thus in both countries, schools tended to ignore it. However, over the last twenty to twenty-five years, attitudes have changed markedly. Holocaust consciousness has reached unparalleled levels and it is thus not surprising that since 1990 the subject has formed part of the National Curriculum in England and Wales. In Canada too, Holocaust education is now widespread. For example, in Ontario, the country's most populous province, there are currently references to the Holocaust in the Grade 10 history curriculum, in English and in courses on world issues, citizenship and human rights. Moreover, in Roman Catholic schools in the province, learning about the Holocaust has been mandatory since 1974. In this chapter we highlight some of the major developments leading to the present situation in the United Kingdom (drawing heavily on Cesarani, 1996) and then chart a similar course in respect of Canada. Our principal aim, though, is to explain the developments and to this end we attempt to identify those factors, both local and global, that since the end of the war have influenced public awareness of the fate of Europe's Jews under the Nazis.

HOLOCAUST EDUCATION IN THE UNITED KINGDOM

The lack of interest in the Holocaust that characterised British society for much of the second half of the twentieth century can be traced back to 1941 when the Ministry of Information decided to play down the Jewish dimension of Nazi atrocities. The government was keen to avoid giving the impression that the war was being fought on behalf of European Jewry. This tendency to obscure the Jewish specificity of the Holocaust continued in the immediate aftermath of the war, as illustrated in Richard Dimbleby's famous report from Belsen for the BBC. In his description of the horrific conditions he witnessed, Jews were mentioned either incidentally or not at all. That this may have been no coincidence is suggested by Tony Kushner (1989:11) who points out that 'Lord Bernstein's official film on the camps, made in 1945, made no reference to the Nazis' extermination programme and consciously removed nearly all references to Jews.' Public awareness of the Holocaust was further eclipsed by the nuclear destruction of Hiroshima and Nagasaki which not only attracted far more media coverage than the enormities of the Nazi regime, but overshadowed the Nuremberg trials of 1946.

For a number of reasons the Holocaust was to remain largely forgotten for the next three decades.

> First, the memory of World War II was so precious and untainted that anything that threatened to disturb this state of affairs was opposed. Second, the universalist liberal framework that dominated British society and culture was resistant to the particularity presented by the Holocaust. And, third, the domination of Englishness and Christianity meant that Jewish marginality was constantly emphasised ... Furthermore, Christians in the post-war world stressed the need for forgiveness and were consequently reluctant to consider the Holocaust in terms of guilt and the apportionment of blame. They continued to ignore Christian responsibility for past and modern anti-Semitism. All three factors combined powerfully after 1945. Both state and public ensured that the history of the Holocaust would remain marginalised and generally neglected.
>
> (Kushner, 1994:277)

Other considerations, however, also played a part in damping down interest in the Holocaust. Among them, according to Cesarani (1996), was the high level of anti-Semitism in the United Kingdom in the immediate post-war years (related to the Palestine emergency). 'It was', he writes, 'an unpropitious atmosphere in which to meditate on the recent past or to seek public commemoration of those who had perished under the Nazis' (p. 618). The murder of two British army officers in Palestine in the summer of 1947 poisoned the atmosphere still further, prompting the editor of a Jewish magazine to observe that because of the Zionist movement, 'the victims of Hitler are being replaced in the popular imagination and sentiment by the victims of the Irgun Zvai Leumi' [a Zionist terror group] (cited in Cesarani, 1996). Anti-Jewish feeling in the United Kingdom, which had led to rioting in a number of towns and cities following the murders, peaked in the winter of 1947/48.

Another partial explanation for the lack of interest in the Holocaust is to be found in the difficulty survivors encountered in making their voices heard. According to Kushner (1995), various factors were responsible. In the first place:

(It) was hard for people to identify on a human level with the survivors. They were portrayed in the media as if they had come from a different planet ... The deathly, marbled figures from the camp newsreels could not be equated with the real people with ordinary needs in Britain.

(Kushner, 1995:161)

Secondly, as already noted, the preciousness of the British war memory sidelined the fate of the Jews. In the words of Auschwitz survivor, Kitty Hart-Moxon:

I was soon to discover that everybody in England would be talking about personal war experiences for months, even years, after hostilities had ceased. But we, who had been pursued over Europe by the mutual enemy and come close to extinction at the hands of that enemy, were not supposed to embarrass people by saying a word.

(Kitty Hart-Moxon, cited in Kushner, 1989:13)

Thirdly, some survivors may have been loath to talk about their experiences due to the prurient nature of the enquiries. This was especially true of young women who were frequently asked about sexual abuse during their incarceration. It was not, in fact, until the 1990s, and specifically, not until the fiftieth anniversary of the liberation of Auschwitz that, according to Anne Karpf (1996:289), 'Holocaust survivors became visible for almost the first time ... They were interviewed on the news, profiled in newspapers, and quoted in an extraordinary, extensive public debate about the concentration camps.'

By all accounts, the Jewish community was no more receptive to the stories of Holocaust survivors than was any other section of British society. For Karpf, the reason was fear within the community that it would be reminded of its failure to act decisively when there was still time to do so.

Survivors ... became begetters of embarrassment who, in a ghastly inversion of expectation and a shocking continuity of the *univers concentrationnaire*, had to be careful not to upset those who hadn't been through the experience: survivors had been transformed from actual sufferers of distress into potential creators of it.

(Karpf, 1996:199)

The tendency for Holocaust survivors to keep their memories to themselves was reflected in the dearth of memoir literature published in the United Kingdom after the war. *The Diary of Anne Frank*, which first appeared in English in 1952, was something of an exception. More typical was the case of Eva Schloss, Anne Frank's step-sister, who only felt able to speak publicly about her experiences forty years after liberation and did not have her autobiography, *Eva's Story*, published until 1988 (Austin, 2000). The virtual absence of survivor testimony had its parallel in the academic world where the first comprehensive history of the Holocaust, Gerald Reitlinger's *The Final Solution*, was not available until 1953. It attracted few reviews. Indeed, Cesarani (*op. cit.*, 622) notes that in the 1950s, 'mainstream British historical scholarship and the memoir literature of British statesmen, diplomats and politicians revealed little awareness of the Final Solution.' Serious attention to subject and to the history of anti-Semitism was largely confined to Jewish émigré writers and Anglo-Jewish historians. Their importance had certainly not filtered through to the writers of school textbooks. According to Cesarani:

> E.J. Passant's widely used student reader *A Short History of Germany 1815-1945*, published in 1959, contained almost nothing on Jews or anti-Semitism. Until the 1960s, British school students learned little about European history after 1918. A survey conducted by the Wiener Library of four textbooks on modern European history showed that they contained no information on anti-Semitism or the Jews.
>
> (Cesarani, 1996:628)

The next decade saw more interest in the Holocaust following the capture of Adolf Eichmann in 1960 and his subsequent trial in Jerusalem, and as a result of the libel action brought by Dr. Dering against Leon Uris, the author of *Exodus*. However, it was not until the 1970s that the Holocaust eventually 'came in from the cold' and it has been suggested that television programmes played a significant part in creating the more receptive climate. Karpf (*op. cit.*) maintains that:

> Jeremy Isaacs' 1975 unsparing television film 'Genocide' in the ITV *World at War* series is credited with beginning the process of introducing the Holocaust into British public consciousness ... But it was the 1978 American TV series *Holocaust* which, though widely derided for its soapiness, properly initiated international public debate. Nevertheless, the Holocaust was still seen as primarily a European experience unconnected with Britain ...
>
> (Karpf, 1996:206-207)

Other television programmes shown in the late 1970s and throughout the 1980s helped to sustain interest in the subject. They included the BBC documentary *Blind Eye to Murder* (1978). Written by Tom Bower, it dealt with British complicity in the escape of Nazi war criminals. The following year saw the airing of *Kitty - Return to Auschwitz* (1979) in which the survivor, Kitty Hart-Moxon, relived her wartime experiences in the presence of her son.

In the arts and literature, as in historical scholarship, the Holocaust did not feature prominently for decades after the event, prompting George Steiner to claim that leading literary figures wrote as though oblivious of the catastrophe that had overtaken the Jews of Europe. In fact, it would be fair to say that the Holocaust did not register in British novels, poetry or drama before the late 1970s. Peter Barnes' play *Auschwitz*, for example, was first staged in 1978 and Thomas Keneally's *Schindler's Ark* was published in 1983.

School textbooks dealing with the history of Nazi Germany began to appear in greater numbers in the 1970s and those we have come across from that time all contain material on the treatment of the Jews. They comment briefly on the anti-Semitic discrimination after 1933, the *Kristallnacht* pogrom of November 1938 and the implementation of the Final Solution. They contain references to the opposition of Christian clerics to the Nazi regime, but no word on the culpability of Christian theology for the Holocaust. They are also silent on Jewish resistance and on non-Jewish rescue and, more often than not, Hitler's other victims are written out of the text. None of the books, for example, mentions the plight of the Jehovah's Witnesses.

Notwithstanding its limited coverage in textbooks, the Holocaust was the focus of a number of travelling displays during the 1980s. For instance, at the start of the decade, the widely admired Polish 'Auschwitz exhibition' toured some of the country's major cities and in London in 1986, the Anne Frank in the World exhibition was unveiled for the first time. [Over the course of the next eleven years, it was to be visited by nearly a million people in locations throughout the United Kingdom.] However, despite the increasing interest in the Holocaust, the subject was not to become a mandatory component of the secondary school history curriculum until 1990.

The National Curriculum

The National Curriculum came into being in England and Wales as a result of the Education Reform Act of 1988. In January 1989, the National Curriculum History Working Group was set up by the government to determine the content of the programmes of study and, controversially, recommended that the rise and fall of Nazi Germany and the Second World War generally, be excluded from the core study units. The decision was justified as follows:

> In making our choice of content we are aware that a number of events of world-historical importance have been excluded. Some omissions ... such as ... the rise and fall of Nazi Germany, could be the subject of School Designed Themes. It has not been our intention to play down the importance of these or other events, but for every suggested addition, something has to make way, and in the process carefully-designed structures may be put at risk.
>
> (Department of Education and Science, 1989:44)

At first sight it would appear that the Holocaust had fallen victim to the Working Group's commitment to placing British history at the heart of its proposals, but whatever the reason, the decision to exclude the Second World War from the curriculum provoked much opposition. [See Rubinstein and Taylor, (1992) for an extended discussion.] Responding to the criticisms of Members of Parliament, ex-servicemen's organisations and educators, the Final Report of the History Working Group, published in April 1990, recommended that study of the

Second World War, including the Holocaust, should be an essential component of the History programme in maintained secondary schools in England and Wales. It was suggested that 14- to 16-year-olds should learn and be assessed on 'the causes of the war; Hitler; casualties of war; Genocide (and) the Holocaust.' However, following the Secretary of State's ruling in 1993 that history was to be an option for this age group, rather than a requirement, the Era of the Second World War became part of Key Stage 3 of the National Curriculum (for 11- to 14-year-olds). A survey of history teachers carried out in the mid-1990s found that the Holocaust was invariably taught (at the end of Year 9) to 13- and 14-year-olds (Short, 1995).

The decision to incorporate the Holocaust into the National Curriculum appears to have caused some apprehension among teachers, judging by Carrie Supple's (1993a) survey of 35 schools in the north-east of England. Based on questionnaire returns and interviews with 28 history teachers, who were mainly Heads of Department, she discovered that many staff felt 'under-informed and under-resourced to teach the subject.' No doubt their unease partly reflected the absence, at the time, of an adequate textbook on the Holocaust available to secondary school teachers in the United Kingdom. Supple found that:

> most textbooks dealt with the Holocaust in a dangerously superficial way. Gaps included few images and little information about Jewish people other than reproductions of anti-Semitic stereotypes; there was no description of the variety of Jewish life before the Holocaust; no explanation of the roots of anti-Semitism; no idea of the variety of responses to Nazism; little on the treatment of minorities under the Nazis other than Jews; no notion of named individuals other than Nazis or perhaps Anne Frank, ... no mention of resistance or 'rescuers'; no mention of the role or responsibility of the 'free world' and no attempt to analyse what made some people into SS murderers, or the combination of factors which enabled the Holocaust (to take place).
>
> (Supple, 1993a:21)

As a result of her research, Supple produced the General Certificate of Secondary Education textbook *From Prejudice to Genocide* (Supple, 1993b), the first book of its kind in the United Kingdom to deal exclusively with Nazi racial policy. Shortly afterwards, the Holocaust Educational Trust sent every secondary school in the country an edited version of Spielberg's *Schindler's List*. Other significant developments over the last decade that reflect the growing interest in Holocaust education include the establishment in 1995 of the Beth Shalom Holocaust memorial and education centre in Nottinghamshire (see Chapter 8); the opening by the Queen in June 2000 of a permanent Holocaust exhibition at the Imperial War Museum in London and the controversial announcement by Prime Minister Tony Blair that, as from January 2001, the United Kingdom was to hold a Holocaust Memorial Day each year on the anniversary of the liberation of Auschwitz (see Cesarani, 2000 and Stone, 2000 for contrasting reactions to the proposal). The country already marks Anne Frank Day which, since its inception in 1996, has seen the participation of over four thousand schools.

Since the 1980s, the Spiro Institute in London (now the London Jewish Cultural Centre) has had as one of its major activities the training of Holocaust educators. Its staff are involved in initial teacher training and mount short courses for those already qualified. In addition, it co-ordinates a nationwide Holocaust survivor programme for secondary schools and publishes resource material. Undertaking very similar work is the Holocaust Educational Trust founded in 1988 as part of the campaign for war crimes legislation. The Trust operates in schools and in institutions of higher education providing teacher training workshops, teaching aids and other classroom resources. It also commissions and disseminates research on Holocaust-related issues. In April 1999 the Trust took 150 teachers (half of them historians) from all over the United Kingdom to Auschwitz-Birkenau and, later in the year, repeated the experience with 170 sixth-form students. These visits now take place annually.

One other institution that deserves to be mentioned in connection with the expansion of Holocaust education in the United Kingdom is the London-based Wiener Library. Although originally established in 1939 as a major archive on Nazi Germany, it has responded to the burgeoning interest in the Holocaust of recent times mainly by providing research facilities and material for academics. However, its education staff also advise teachers on the use of resources and give talks to schools and colleges.

THE HISTORY OF HOLOCAUST EDUCATION IN CANADA

Holocaust consciousness in Canada followed a similar trajectory from shadow to light, as did Holocaust awareness in the United Kingdom. There are, however, some major differences in the factors that explain developments in the two countries. Chief among them is the size and vitality of the survivor community in Canada, the adoption of multiculturalism as part of the national legislative framework and the fact that the country has always been sensitive to the hegemonic influence of the United States. Because of the importance of the latter we will provide an overview of the broader North American socio-political context before taking into account the unique set of circumstances that have helped shape the evolution of Holocaust education in Canada.

The Broader North American Framework

In North America, Holocaust consciousness began to emerge in the 1970s after a prolonged gestation period. In fact, the word 'Holocaust' was not commonly used before the end of the 1950s and it was not until 1968 that the American Library of Congress created a major entry card for the Holocaust. Commenting on this lengthy period of occlusion, Canada's pre-eminent Holocaust historian, Michael Marrus, remarked that during his historical training in the mid-1960s: 'the Holocaust was simply absent ... No one would have thought to mention it in a lecture' (Marrus, 1995:27). He pointed out that: 'In 1953, a distinguished historian at the University of Toronto wrote a modern history of Germany without referring to (the Holocaust) at all and in this, I hasten to add, historians reflected (its) wider absence in the culture of the day' (*ibid.*). The neglect continued for decades as evidenced by the treatment of the subject in textbooks used in Canadian schools. One study found that out of 72 history books dealing with the modern world that were in use in Canada in the early 1980s, half had nothing, or less than a paragraph, on the Holocaust (Glickman and Bardikoff, 1982).

In the United States, the lack of interest in the subject that persisted throughout the 1950s, has been attributed to a number of factors and not least to the cold war which required that the Soviet Union be equated, in terms of totalitarian terror, with Hitler's Germany. As Novick (*op. cit.*, 87) puts it: 'any suggestion that the Nazi murder of European Jewry was a central, let alone defining, feature of that regime would undermine the argument for the essential identity of the two systems.' Another factor that partly explains the lack of attention paid to the Holocaust in North America during this period is that the established Jewish community was primarily concerned with relief, restitution and the absorption of Holocaust survivors and their families. For a long time, the community was preoccupied with re-establishing a sense of normalcy and thus had no opportunity to respond collectively to the enormity of the Holocaust. It has further been suggested that, as in the United Kingdom, American Jews were not especially interested in listening to survivors recount their experiences (Bartov, 1998). Indeed, those who managed to find refuge in the United States were often discouraged from dwelling on the past (Wyman, 1996b). And again, in common with the United Kingdom, the silence of survivors in the States was compounded by a dearth of both academic and popular literature on the Holocaust that lasted until the early 1960s.

The event that began to dislodge the Holocaust from the shadows was the Eichmann trial and Hannah Arendt's incendiary commentary on its proceedings published first in *The New Yorker* and then in the book, *Eichmann in Jerusalem* (Arendt, 1963). The controversy that followed the trial, and Arendt's report, assisted in the emergence of 'a distinct thing called the Holocaust – an event in its own right' (Novick, *op. cit.*, 144); consciousness of the Holocaust had begun to crystallise. An additional factor contributing at this time to the change in attitude towards the Holocaust as a 'war within a war,' was the publication of a number of other books and one highly-publicised play that helped inform the American public of the fate of European Jewry and the genocidal aim of the Nazis. Prior to the 1960s, very little had been written on the Holocaust, and with the exception of Anne Frank's heavily edited *Diary of a Young Girl*, the little that was available had a limited readership. The break with the past came in the form of Raul Hilberg's *The Destruction of the European Jews* which appeared in 1961. It was published in the middle of the Eichmann trial and attracted widespread attention largely on account of its disdain for Jewish passivity. The stage play that drew much interest was *The Deputy* written by the German Protestant, Rolf Hochhuth. Highly critical of the role of Pius XII in the murder of the Jews, the production opened on Broadway in 1964. It was performed at around the same time as survivor memoirs started to appear. Jean Améry's (1980) *At the Mind's Limits* (first published in 1966), Viktor Frankl's (1962) *Man's Search for Meaning*, and Primo Levi's (1987) *If This is a Man*, (originally published in 1947 and re-issued in 1958) contributed to a significant body of literary work that made the general reading public aware of the horrors visited upon European Jewry.

Against this backdrop of newly acquired or newly acknowledged information occurred a sequence of events in the Middle East that acted as a powerful catalyst in defining the relationship of North American Jews to the Holocaust. The first of these galvanizing events was the period leading up to the Six Day War. In Arthur Hertzberg's words: 'As soon as the Arab armies began to mass on the borders of Israel during the third week in May 1967, the mood of the American Jewish community underwent an abruptly radical and possibly permanent change' (Hertzberg, 1979:210). In the build-up to the war, Jews became acutely aware that the existence and safety of Israel was viscerally important to them. One result of this keenly felt anxiety was that they saw themselves cut-off from mainstream North American culture and looked to one another, as Jews, for understanding and support. They had become, seemingly in an instant, strong and resolute as a community, intensely aware of their vulnerability as Jews and ardently committed to the survival of Israel.

The response of the North American Jewish community to the Holocaust itself had been to work quietly through diplomatic channels and not to act in any way that would seem openly to question government policies. They did not want to exacerbate inadvertently the anti-Semitism which was so close to the surface of American life in the 1930s and 1940s. After the facts of the Holocaust became known, there was much guilt within the community for not having responded in an unequivocal way that may have saved more lives. In the anxious weeks prior to the Six-Day War, Jews found themselves both ready and determined to face the perceived threat to their survival. They were in a position to act decisively because in the post-war years they had been able to create both a solid economic and political base. To meet Israel's urgent need for arms, American Jewry mounted the largest and most successful fundraising campaign in its history, amassing US $100 million in three weeks (Hertzberg, 1979). This immediate and effective response to a new threat, this re-writing of the past by symbolically repeating it and yet changing the outcome, allowed the community a chance to redeem itself in its own eyes.

When the Six-Day War was surprisingly and stunningly won, a new sense of pride in Jewish heritage was born. It was no longer necessary to repress knowledge about the Holocaust as it could now be experienced through more recent historical events in which Jews had not only survived but emerged victorious. Had there been no victory it would be hard to say if the Holocaust would have been so readily embraced as a symbol of Jewish identity. Hence the events surrounding the Six-Day War did much to liberate the Holocaust from the repressed unconscious of the North American Jewish community and to place it at the forefront of Jewish iconography. Holocaust consciousness had moved from the margins to the centre. Wyman (1996b:727) points out that 'in the aftermath of the 1967 and 1973 wars, American Jews made determined efforts to extend knowledge of the Holocaust not only within the Jewish community but also to the wider society.'

The other major factor that facilitated an awareness of the Holocaust in North America was the television mini-series *Holocaust*. The nine-and-a-half hour drama was broadcast by NBC on four consecutive evenings in April 1978 and was watched by close to 120 million people. Among other things, it dealt with the Nuremberg Laws, *Kristallnacht*, the Wannsee Conference, Babi Yar, the Warsaw Ghetto uprising, the concentration camps and the sites of mass murder. The airing of this series created a well-spring of interest in the Holocaust throughout the continent and in some ways marks the beginning of Holocaust education in both the United States and Canada.

Canada

Thus far, we have discussed events that affected North American society as a whole. Canada, however, had a distinct set of circumstances that distilled these larger events into its own particular response. They included a growing social and cultural pluralism and public policies that were formulated to accommodate the country's increasing diversity. [See Bialystok (2000) for a comprehensive historical analysis.]

Canada has always been a heterogeneous society. Prior to European contacts, the indigenous population comprised around fifty distinct sub-cultures and over twelve languages. In the sixteenth and seventeenth centuries there was an influx of French fur traders followed by the British who eventually outnumbered the French. To these three founding peoples came wave after wave of immigrants who dramatically altered the ethnic composition of the population, especially after the Second World War. To acknowledge and respond to this increasing diversity, the government, under Prime Minister Pierre Trudeau, declared a federal policy commitment to the principles of multiculturalism. The Multiculturalism Act of 1971 asserted that 'there is no official culture, nor does any ethnic group take precedence over any other' (Troper, 1991). Thus, ethnicity was not only recognised as an integral feature of Canadian society, but 'ethnocultural preservation and growth became goals of public policy' (*ibid.*). One of the consequences of these political changes was that the late 1970s and early 1980s witnessed the development of many educational curricula dealing with multiculturalism. Courses that celebrated the culture and history of Canada's ethnic groups and those that promoted prejudice reduction were encouraged and, just as importantly, generously funded by local school boards. They created an educational milieu that was very receptive to Holocaust education, for the latter was also seen as a means of combating discrimination and promoting respect for cultural diversity. A special issue of the *History and Social Science Teacher* in 1986 paid testimony to its contribution.

As suggested earlier, one of the reasons why Holocaust education became a rallying point for Canadian Jews, in contrast to the situation in the United Kingdom, was the size and vitality of the survivor community, principally in Toronto and Montreal. Partly as a result, Holocaust education, especially in areas where survivors were prominent, developed sooner, to a greater extent and at a faster rate than in the United Kingdom. We turn next to highlight the survivor-led activities that helped shape Holocaust education in Canada. We focus primarily on educational activities in Ontario, the province where most survivors settled, as space does not permit us to detail parallel developments in other parts of the country.

Educational Initiatives

One manifestation of the increasing interest in Holocaust commemoration was the establishment of the National Holocaust Remembrance Committee of the Canadian Jewish Congress in 1973. By 1976, local Remembrance Committees, most of whose members were survivors, were active in twelve Canadian cities and particularly in Toronto. In 1978, the Toronto Jewish Congress, in response to both the television mini-series on the Holocaust and a seminal teachers' conference, started a Holocaust education committee staffed by survivors, teachers who were the children of survivors and a number of educators interested in multiculturalism. Its activities included Summer Teacher Training Institutes, long-term collaboration with local school boards, the production of two Holocaust education curricula, professional development for teachers, lecture series and perhaps, most notably, the creation of an annual student seminar day on the Holocaust in Toronto which continues to attract in the region of 600 to 900 participants. Similar large venue student seminars take place annually in other cities in Ontario and in Vancouver B.C. More than two decades after its inception, the Toronto Seminar has reached in excess of 18,000 high-school students.

Another major advance in the goal to educate Canadians about the Holocaust was the creation of at least four museums in the country. The Holocaust Education and Memorial Centre of Toronto is the largest and was opened in 1985. [A more detailed description of its mandate and work will be found in Chapter 8.] A very different educational initiative that has had a significant impact on public awareness is the Holocaust Education Week in Toronto, first held in 1981. This public education programme takes place each year around the time of *Kristallnacht* and Canada's Remembrance Day. In recent years, well over a hundred events have been scheduled including lectures from internationally renowned Holocaust historians and other scholars, dramatic presentations, survivor testimonies, films and commemorations. The events, sponsored by the Toronto Holocaust Education and Memorial Centre (now the Holocaust Centre of Toronto) take place in synagogues, churches, libraries, universities and community centres and, to the best of our knowledge, constitute the largest annual public educational initiative on the Holocaust in the world.

A further project of national significance has been the Holocaust and Hope Educational Programme under the auspices of the League for Human Rights of B'nai Brith. It began in 1986, partly in response to the publicity surrounding two court cases involving Holocaust denial. James Keegstra, a history teacher and mayor of a small town in Alberta, had for years been instructing his students that the Holocaust was an exaggeration perpetrated by Jews and he had failed students who dared to disagree with him. A non-Jewish parent filed a successful suit against Keegstra under Canada's anti-hate Laws. As a result, he was fired from his job, but succeeded in appealing the decision all the way to the Supreme Court where the conviction was upheld. At around the same time, another Holocaust denier, Ernst Zündel, was charged under the false news section of the Criminal Code. Although found guilty in the lower courts, the Supreme Court quashed his conviction as unconstitutional. Both cases raised concern over the apparent rise in Holocaust denial and underscored the need for ongoing Holocaust education (Mock, 2000). The education programme that the League for Human Rights developed in the wake of these two cases intends 'to have teachers confront history and to become witnesses themselves' (*ibid.*). The programme involves a three-week tour to Germany, Poland and Israel. On their return, participants living in the greater Toronto area are invited to join a committee that concentrates on giving professional support to colleagues interested in teaching about the Holocaust and human rights. Although the League is based in Toronto, the net for teachers is cast wide and those who enrol are chosen, to some extent, on a regional basis from across the country. As a result, over the last decade and a half, more than 150 teachers and educators nationwide have participated. The project has recently expanded so that on alternate years, the League now takes multi-faith high school students from all parts of Canada on an educational journey to Poland and Israel. A similar educational project ('March of the Living') caters to Jewish students.

Although these travel programmes are widely regarded as successful in acquainting students and teachers with historical knowledge, they have been criticised for politicising Holocaust education. The emotional impact of visiting Israel immediately after Auschwitz does make the existence of the Jewish state seem an uncomplicated moral and political imperative. The relationship between the Holocaust and the establishment of Israel is a significant one, but is not as simple and linear as a three-hour flight from Warsaw to Tel Aviv would suggest. The March of the Living has also been criticised on pedagogic grounds. It has been argued that adolescents often lack the critical faculties required to assimilate the catastrophic results of the Holocaust without running the risk of internalising a potentially destructive identification with victimhood.

Within the past few years, one of the most promising, but ultimately disappointing initiatives in Holocaust education in Ontario has been a collaborative graduate certificate course in Holocaust and Genocide Education. It was spearheaded by the Holocaust Centre of Toronto and a small group of academics at the University of Toronto. The purpose of the course was to train teachers of Holocaust and genocide-related subjects, support classroom-based research on effective pedagogies, host international conferences and fund internships for Holocaust and genocide scholars, especially those from countries that have recently experienced mass, state-sponsored violence. The programme ran for two years but was aborted for financial reasons. It is thought that some anticipated donations failed to materialise because of tensions arising from the Israeli-Palestinian conflict; not least, the perceived affinity that left-wing academics have with anti-Israeli sentiments.

Provincial Legislation

Ontario has also seen the enactment of provincial legislation to proclaim Holocaust Memorial Day (Yom Ha-Shoah). The draft legislation (Bill 66), was the first of its kind in Canada, although Quebec and British Columbia are presently considering something similar. The bill, which received its first reading in October 1998, was clearly set in a broad human rights and multicultural framework, for the preamble states that:

> It is appropriate to establish a Holocaust Memorial Day - Yom Ha-Shoah - in Ontario to commemorate the victims of the Holocaust of 1933-1945. Such a day would provide an opportunity to reflect on and educate about the enduring lessons

of the Holocaust. This day shall also provide an opportunity to consider other instances of systematic destruction of peoples, human rights issues and the multicultural reality of modern society.

Notwithstanding its landmark status, the educational significance of Bill 66 remains in doubt. It did not mandate Holocaust education; nor was it accompanied, despite government indications to the contrary, by a provincially backed Holocaust curriculum or educational package.

In conclusion, it would appear that certain international events, notably the Eichmann trial and the televising of *Holocaust*, have played a crucial role in the evolution of Holocaust education in both the United Kingdom and Canada. Factors specific to each country have also assumed a key role and here we have in mind the fillip provided by the Multiculturalism Act in Canada and the inhibitory impact of post-war anti-Semitism in the United Kingdom. However, the single most important determinant of the genesis and development of Holocaust education in both countries seems to have been the level of activity of the survivor community. It is no coincidence that Holocaust consciousness was at its lowest ebb during the period when survivors' voices, for whatever reason, met with a stony silence. Conversely, it is not just happenstance that accounts for Holocaust education having started earlier and progressed further in Canada than in the United Kingdom. The explanation is to be found, to a large extent, in the integral role in Holocaust education played by Canadian survivors from the beginning. As we have seen, they formed the core of the country's many Holocaust Remembrance Committees and were the generating force behind the establishment of the most prominent memorial museums.

Chapter 3

Antiracist Education and the Holocaust

Much publicity was given to antiracist education in Canada and the United Kingdom in the 1990s following the 1992 riots in Toronto and the inquiry into the murder in London in 1993 of the black teenager Stephen Lawrence (Macpherson, 1999). However, the movement for antiracist education had emerged and attained a degree of prominence during the previous decade. It developed in the United Kingdom in the early 1980s and somewhat later in Canada as a response to the perceived inadequacies of multiculturalism. Carrington and Short (1989) outline the differences between the two perspectives as follows:

> The goal of multicultural education is to foster mutual understanding and tolerance by changing the perceptions and attitudes of individuals through a pluralist programme of curricular reform. The sympathetic portrayal of a range of cultures and lifestyles ... is seen as benefiting all pupils ... In contrast, antiracists are primarily concerned with differences in life chances rather than lifestyles and (particularly concerned with) the structural basis of racism and racial inequality in schools and society at large.
>
> (Carrington and Short, 1989:12)

From the outset, one of the major failings of antiracist education, in our view, has been its consistent neglect of the Holocaust. This lack of interest in how the subject is taught is a source of regret and a matter of some disquiet, for while the Holocaust has the potential to further the aims of antiracist education, it also has the potential to undermine them. The outcome ought not to be left to chance; but before antiracist educators can be persuaded to take an active interest in how the Holocaust is handled in schools, they must first be convinced of its relevance to the realisation of their goals. We therefore begin this chapter by considering some of the ways in which a study of the Holocaust can both reinforce and extend the achievements of conventional antiracism (which aims to overcome the problems faced by visible minorities). We then discuss various ways in which teaching the Holocaust can go wrong and show how, in the course of going wrong, it can threaten the entire antiracist project. In the second part of the chapter, we attempt to account for the antiracist neglect of the Holocaust in both the United Kingdom and Canada.

Reinforcing and Advancing the aims of Antiracist Education

Antiracist education is concerned, among other things, with the nature of stereotyping and with how the process serves to justify discriminatory behaviour. If students are to understand the concept of a stereotype, rather than simply come to recognise particular manifestations within a given social formation, it would be useful for them to encounter the concept in as many different guises as possible. A study of Nazi Germany, with an emphasis on the Holocaust, is self-evidently helpful in this respect, for the topic offers an opportunity to examine not just anti-Semitic stereotypes, but those relating to a range of victim groups. Moreover, an exploration of the Nazi era allows students to learn that while negative stereotyping of minorities does not always take the same form, or have the same provenance, it always has the same consequence; namely, the establishment of a psychological climate in which racial, ethnic, religious and other kinds of enmity can flourish.

Antiracist educators are also concerned to apprise students of the nature of scapegoating. While those who focus exclusively on the situation of visible minorities in the United Kingdom and Canada should have no difficulty in promoting this understanding, there is plainly no British or Canadian equivalent to the social, economic and psychological dislocation that afflicted Germany between the wars and the search for scapegoats that that dislocation engendered. The Jewish experience in Germany in the years preceding Hitler's accession to power provides a particularly graphic illustration of the scapegoating process and, as such, constitutes a further reason for treating the Holocaust as a potent weapon in the antiracist armoury.

In addition to its role in supporting the contribution made by antiracist educators, awareness of the Holocaust can make a distinctive contribution to the promotion of antiracism. Most obviously, as was pointed out in Chapter 1, this will involve leaving students in no doubt as to where racism can lead, no matter how sophisticated the society it infects. Students may find it easy enough to conceptualise racism in terms of name-calling, social and economic discrimination, physical assault and even the occasional murder, but wholesale destruction of an entire people as an officially sanctioned industrial process, is unlikely to be imagined, let alone understood, unless it is deliberately taught. If students are familiarised with the horror of the *Einsatzgruppen* and the death camps and are helped to see the horror as the ultimate expression of racist ideology, they may become more sensitive to, and concerned about, levels of racism they would previously have overlooked as trivial.

A less obvious advantage of learning about the Holocaust relates to what may be considered a major flaw in conventional antiracist education. This is the assumption that people behave, or are likely to behave, in racist ways because they lack relevant knowledge. The problem, as antiracists see it, is not ignorance of other cultures, the key premise of multicultural education, but rather ignorance of racism itself. As Troyna and Williams (1986) put it:

> Antiracists ... argue for policy initiatives designed to change *institutions* rather than children. These include the politicisation of the formal curriculum ... As numerous books and pamphlets have indicated, a politicised curriculum would discuss the origins and manifestations of racism and would be directed as much to white as (to) black students.
>
> (Troyna and Williams, 1986:47. Original emphasis)

While common sense might suggest that knowledge of the history of racism and its contemporary manifestations would result in a lessening of racist behaviour, there is no evidence that it does so. Indeed, there is good reason to believe that for many students, an increased understanding of racism, even if it helps to change attitudes, will have no bearing on behaviour, for the cost of acting in accordance with our conscience can be prohibitive. The price we pay for challenging racism might be social, in the form of ostracism by the peer group, or physical, as was the case during the Holocaust when those who sought to assist Jews were faced with the prospect of death. The issue that antiracists need to address, therefore, is not just that of deciding the content most likely to foster an understanding of racism; they must also consider measures aimed at helping students to *act* against racism regardless of pressures to act otherwise. One means of doing this may be to encourage them to re-conceptualise, or at least to broaden, their notion of a hero so as to include those who are prepared to stand up for what they believe to be right no matter what the personal cost. [Revamping the notion in this way naturally assumes that the course of action to be pursued is a morally acceptable one.] In the mid-1990s, history teachers in the United Kingdom were urged by some influential educationists (notably by Dr. Nicholas Tate, Chief Executive of the School Curriculum and Assessment Authority) to venerate the country's traditional heroes - men and women who, in one way or another, served the nation well (see, for example, *The Times*, September 18, 1995). While not wishing to belittle or derogate the contribution of these individuals, or deny them the posthumous glory to which they are entitled, we note that their claim to fame rarely rests on their resisting pressure to adopt a position they regarded as dishonourable. And when, to a greater or lesser extent, it does, as with Winston Churchill during the 'wilderness years,' it is not that aspect of their reputation which is lauded as heroic. In contrast, the history of the Holocaust contains numerous examples of ordinary individuals who were willing to make the ultimate sacrifice for the sake of doing what they knew to be right; they defied authority in order to offer protection to Jews and other persecuted minorities. Thus, in celebrating the exploits of rescuers such as Miep Gies, one of a small group who looked after the Frank family in Amsterdam, and those less well-known like Albert Bedane in the Channel Islands, we may be helping to create a moral climate conducive to the struggle against racism more generally.

Obviating the Drawbacks of Antiracist Education

Antiracist education faces a number of potential difficulties, one of which, according to David Gillborn (1995), stems from the need to go beyond permeation, that is, the incorporation of antiracism into all areas of the curriculum. Gillborn maintains that:

> Even in schools where all subject departments take seriously their duty to address antiracist issues it may be necessary to supplement this with additional work. Certain issues ... cannot be fully explored within the limited time and material resources available to core and other foundation subjects in the National Curriculum ... Additionally ... there is a tendency for antiracist materials and ideas to be used only if the opportunity arises via more familiar subject-specific concerns or materials. In this way, without proper co-ordination between and within subjects, antiracism may appear to be incidental to the 'real' work of the group and occur in haphazard ways ... threatening its credibility in the eyes of students.
>
> (Gillborn, 1995:133)

Where such difficulties exist, Gillborn has urged that antiracism be given its own explicit space within the curriculum. To illustrate, he refers to an all-girls' multiracial secondary school in central England that created 'a people's education programme' with the aim of addressing 'issues of power and exclusion in society.' It was introduced as a dimension of the personal and social education of all the students, but it is precisely because antiracism is not recognised as a traditional subject that initiatives of this kind may be perceived by some white students as artificial. In so far as they are perceived in this way, there is a risk, especially at secondary school level, of their being seen as a crude attempt to convert rather than educate. Put simply, they may be construed as a form of preaching rather than teaching. The psychological concept of reactance (Brehm, 1966) suggests that students who interpret the situation in this light will be motivated to resist the message, perhaps going so far as to adopt a stance diametrically opposed to it. The reason, according to Brehm, is that we all have a fundamental need to see ourselves as autonomous, that is, as having the power to make our own decisions. Any perceived attempt to restrict that freedom (such as pressure to embrace an antiracist point of view) will be resented and, in all probability, rejected, in order that we may regain a sense of control over our own destiny. Other things being equal, there is little danger of reactance arising in respect of the Holocaust for, as we have argued, apart from a small band of right-wing extremists, the attempted genocide of the Jews of Europe is universally acknowledged to have been a major component of Nazi policy during the Second World War.

A second problem with antiracist education that knowledge of the Holocaust is able to obviate relates to the fact that in both the United Kingdom (as distinct from most European states) and in Canada, students can learn about the systematic murder of millions relatively free from guilt. This may not be the case when they learn about racism in their own country. Indeed, with reference to the situation in the United Kingdom, James Lynch (1987:x) has characterised antiracist education as 'political, confrontational and guilt-inducing in its approach.' Guilt is not conducive to learning; quite the reverse. It is experienced as an unpleasant emotion that the ego attempts to defend itself against by such means as denial or blaming the victim. That British and Canadian students may be able to confront the Holocaust with little or no remorse is suggested by the comparative ease with which they can distance themselves from it in terms of time and space. [That said, they should not be led to conclude that their own countries' response to Nazi anti-Semitism was beyond reproach. The pre-war policy of both governments towards Jewish refugees has been seen by a number of commentators as itself partly motivated by anti-Semitism.]

Yet another disadvantage of conventional antiracism is that its message may well be spurned by students who are involved in racist sub-cultures (e.g. Willis, 1977). Plainly, the issue of guilt does not arise in such cases, for the problem is rather one of ideological opposition. These students will very likely make a conscious decision to reject what they are being taught simply because it is at variance with their basic beliefs. Now in so far as disaffected youth embrace anti-Semitism less enthusiastically than they embrace what Tariq Modood (1992) refers to as 'colour racism' - and there can be little doubt, despite the reverberations of the crisis in the Middle East, that the latter is currently the more serious problem - they may be more receptive to learning about racism via the Holocaust than via something 'nearer home,' Indeed, they may be especially receptive to learning about the Holocaust if, as a result of their racist sympathies, they have acquired some sort of misguided reverence for those who instigated it. [Nathan (2003) has recently reported evidence of the beneficial impact that a visit to Auschwitz can have on the racial attitudes of young people who had previously evinced hostile feelings towards ethnic minorities.]

We turn, finally, to a very different reason for antiracists involving themselves in teaching about the Holocaust and that is the need to ensure that the topic is taught in a manner that does not compromise, or diminish in any way, the achievements of those working within the conventional antiracist fold. The scope for such a detrimental impact is considerable. It could result, for instance, from teachers inadvertently portraying the 'racial' victims of Nazism in a negative light - as in some sense deserving their fate. If that were the case, racism, in all its forms, would not only be rendered comprehensible to some extent but, in the process, would acquire a degree of social and intellectual respectability. Such unintentional maligning of victims could ensue from teachers responding inappropriately to anti-Semitic or racist remarks, or from them simply conveying their own ignorance of the Holocaust and of events connected with it. A further danger resides in the amount of time devoted to the subject. Too little might encourage students to think of the Holocaust, and by extension, all forms of racism, as a relatively inconsequential matter; too much might breed resentment against what is seen as undue pressure and lead, via reactance, to a rejection of the message. The time factor would appear to be particularly important in England and Wales at present, because while schools have to teach the Holocaust as an aspect of world history, they have discretion as to whether they cover it in outline or in depth.

While we have shown that antiracist educators have good reason to take an active interest in the teaching of the Holocaust, in both the United Kingdom and in Canada they have manifestly failed to do so. In the remainder of this chapter we attempt to account for the neglect.

EXPLAINING THE NEGLECT IN THE UNITED KINGDOM

The reluctance of the antiracist movement to engage with the Holocaust might be explained, to some extent, by the fact that, as we have seen, British society tended to sideline the Holocaust for much of the post-war period. We noted in the previous chapter Anne Karpf's comments about the significance of television programmes in the 1970s, and particularly the genocide episode of the *World at War* series, in stimulating interest in the subject among the British public. Even so, as Karpf observes, it was not until 1983 that the country erected its first memorial to the Holocaust, a 'small and unobtrusive ... garden' in London's Hyde Park.

Although the long-standing and widespread indifference of British society to the fate of the Jews during the Nazi era may partially explain the antiracist neglect of the Holocaust, other factors need to be taken into account. It has to be recognised, for example, that from the beginning, the antiracist movement has shown a conspicuous lack of interest in anti-Semitism. Indeed, it is the apparent unconcern of antiracists for this form of prejudice that offers the most plausible explanation for their continuing failure to come to terms with the Holocaust. To account for their unwillingness to take up the cudgels on behalf of anti-Semitism, it is sometimes suggested that for antiracists, Jews are not even seen as an ethnic minority. [The journalist, Melanie Phillips (1996), argues along these lines in her withering critique of liberal orthodoxies in education, *All Must Have Prizes.*] But whatever the antiracist perception of the Jewish community, the fact remains that anti-Semitism has historically been excluded from the antiracist agenda and, as was pointed out just over a decade ago, the extent of the exclusion can be judged by the dearth of references to the subject in mainstream antiracist literature (Short, 1991b). Little seems to have changed in the intervening period, despite the greater attention paid to the Holocaust by British society as a whole. Certainly, major publications in the field of antiracist education over the last ten years make almost no mention of Jews or of anti-Semitism. This is true, to give just two examples, of David Gillborn's (1995) *Racism and Antiracism in Real Schools* and the late Barry Troyna's (1993) *Racism and Education*. The virtual absence of any reference to anti-Semitism in these books is of particular significance because of the standing of the two authors within the antiracist movement. Troyna's failure to take anti-Semitism seriously is especially surprising in view of his definition of racism as embracing groups distinguished by either physical or cultural characteristics (Troyna and Carrington, 1990). It is even more surprising in the light of his own experiences, for in the Preface to *Racism and Education* he writes about the difficulties he encountered as a Jewish schoolboy from local racist gangs and claims to recollect, among other things, the burning of synagogues.

A further way to account for the antiracist neglect of anti-Semitism would be to contend that antiracists no longer regard hostility towards Jews as a problem; that in the words of Robert Jeffcoate (1984:7), anti-Semitism is 'almost, but not quite, a nightmare of the past.' Now in so far as the 'no problem' thesis is responsible for antiracism's failure to take anti-Semitism seriously, the prospects for a change of policy are encouraging, for there are good grounds for thinking that such a thesis is unduly sanguine. Admittedly, anti-Semitism in the United Kingdom today is less of a problem than it used to be and such difficulties as Jews currently face do not begin to compare with those of the African-Caribbean and South Asian communities. None the less, as a 1994 report from the Runnymede Trust made clear:

> Between 1984 and 1992 there had been an 85% increase in the reporting of anti-Semitic incidents - incidents such as physical attacks on Jewish individuals, desecration of Jewish cemeteries, arson attacks on Jewish property and daubing of graffiti on Jewish buildings. In the same period there was an increase in the dissemination of virulent anti-Semitic pamphlets and books, and in abusive anti-Semitic literature sent through the post to Jewish individuals and organisations.
> (Runnymede Trust, 1994:11)

More recently, Robert Wistrich (1999:29) has claimed that anti-Semitism 'in Britain continues to fester quietly beneath the surface as part of the more widespread antagonism to all those minorities who deviate from mainstream definitions of 'Englishness'.' And neo-Nazi literature, of course, persists in promoting the Hitlerian image of the Jew as a corrosive parasite intent on undermining the state in the interests of an international conspiracy. The establishment of Israel and the policies of recent Israeli governments, needless to say, have done nothing to dissolve or soften this image. They have merely re-shaped it, for the epithet of 'brutal occupier' can now be added to the litany of indictments. [See Iganski and Kosmin, (2003) for an extended discussion of the links between the Middle East conflict and the recrudescence of anti-Semitism.] While it is doubtful whether this stereotype of the Jew, *in toto* or in part, has much appeal beyond the constituency of the extreme-right and fundamentalist Muslim groups, it has to be acknowledged that despite periodic remission, the cancer of anti-Semitism has yet to be eradicated from the European mindset. It has proved to be the most durable of prejudices and for this reason we should heed Conor Cruise O'Brien's description of it as 'a very light sleeper' (cited in Runnymede Trust, 1994).

The distancing of antiracists from anti-Semitism could also be explained if it were the case that a significant number of antiracists were themselves anti-Semitic, rejecting all forms of racial and ethnic prejudice but making an exception in the case of Jews. While acknowledging the absence of any hard evidence in support of this hypothesis, it is, perhaps, worth recalling that antiracism is far from unknown in left-wing circles; indeed, a minority of luminaries within the Socialist pantheon have been noted for their overt hostility towards Jews. In pride of place is Karl Marx whose two review essays *On the Jewish Question* (published in 1844) arguably stand as the *locus classicus* of Socialist anti-Semitism.

Writing on the historic connection between anti-Semitism and the Left, Bernard Lewis (1987) maintains that:

> One article (by Marx) speaks of the Polish Jews as 'that dirtiest of all races ...' In Marx's view, Jews were not only responsible for capitalism, but even for sometimes strongly anti-Semitic capitalistic governments: 'We find every tyrant backed by a Jew as is every Pope by a Jesuit. In truth, the craving of oppressors would be hopeless and the practicability of war out of the question if there was not an army of Jesuits to smother thought and a handful of Jews to ransack pockets.
>
> (Lewis, 1987:112)

Similar sentiments have been expressed by other major figures on the Left. Consequently, one ought not to rule out the possibility of anti-Semitism playing a part in the failure of some antiracists to concern themselves with Jewish insecurities. However, an explanation in terms of anti-Semitism is implausible when trying to account for the widespread nature of the neglect, for the central finding from studies of the prejudiced personality (e.g. Adorno *et al.*, 1950) is that anti-Semitic individuals are unlikely to be drawn in large numbers to a movement that campaigns actively on behalf of *any* ethnic minority. Moreover, talk of anti-Semitism is hardly convincing when one bears in mind the substantial representation of Jews within the antiracist movement.

While personal animosity might not be able to account for the antiracist indifference to anti-Semitism, long-established hostility towards Israel by the Left in general might be thought more credible. Over the past thirty years or so, there has been even less sympathy for the Jewish state from this political quarter than from society-at-large and those on the Left have, perhaps, been inclined to tar the Jewish community with guilt by association. As Kushner (1989:14) has written: 'To large sections of the left-liberal world in Britain, the Jew remains the oppressor rather than the oppressed' - a claim that has, from time to time, aroused considerable controversy; witness the 1987 play *Perdition* by the Trotskyite Jim Allen and the recent cartoon in Britain's *Independent* newspaper (January 27, 2003) showing Israeli Prime Minister, Ariel Sharon, biting off the bloodied head of a Palestinian child.

The explanations considered so far for antiracists ignoring anti-Semitism (and thus the Holocaust) relate to the beliefs and attitudes of individual antiracists. In contrast, the final explanation to be discussed is suggested by the nature of antiracism itself and specifically by its commitment to eradicating both individual prejudice *and* all forms of racial inequality. This double-barrelled focus does not just distinguish multicultural from antiracist education; it is also the source of a dilemma that has arguably inhibited antiracists from engaging with anti-Semitism. Essentially, antiracists define racism as 'prejudice plus power' and whatever quibbles some of them may have with this definition, they all see racism working against the interests of the black and Asian population in favour of the white majority. Debbie Epstein (1993), for example, maintains that racism results in 'black disadvantage in housing, employment, education and many other areas of everyday life ... while conferring advantage on white people ...' (p. 16). Antiracists can comfortably accommodate any ethnic or racial minority exposed to both individual prejudice and institutional discrimination. They have a problem, however, when a minority suffers from prejudice but is not otherwise disadvantaged. The problem is thrown into particularly sharp relief when the group concerned is widely perceived as powerful (no matter how temporary this state of affairs may be). In such a situation the predicament that confronts antiracists is to know whether or not to respond to the prejudice. For if, as is likely, the elimination or diminution of the prejudice results in the group concerned becoming even more powerful, antiracists would find themselves aggravating the very inequality they are pledged to undermine. If, on the other hand, they fail to respond, they effectively collude with racism and thereby contradict their *raison d'être*.

The present position of the Jewish community in the United Kingdom exemplifies the antiracist dilemma *par excellence*. For as various writers have remarked (e.g. Brook, 1989; Cesarani, 2003), there can be little doubt that Jews play a prominent part in the arts, the professions and commerce and are also well represented in the Establishment. For example, out of a community variously estimated at around 300,000, there have, in recent times, been as many as 46 Jewish members of Parliament (in 1974) and five Jewish Cabinet Ministers (in 1983). And in the sphere of education, the Jewish community again would seem much better placed than many other minorities. Jewish teachers are thought to be adequately represented at all levels of the profession and, unlike the African-Caribbean and some Asian groups, concern has never been expressed about Jewish children's educational attainments. Indeed, as long ago as 1902-3, the Royal Commission on Alien Immigration was flattering in its assessment of their ability to learn.

ANTI-RACIST EDUCATION AND THE HOLOCAUST:
THE CANADIAN PERSPECTIVE

In Canada, the emergence of multicultural and then antiracist education was largely a response to the rapid diversification of the population base that escalated during the post-war period and continues apace. Although multiethnic classrooms have existed in urban areas throughout the country since the 1950s, the schools in some of these locations today are marked by an unprecedented degree of diversity. This was evident in the 1997 *Every Secondary Student Survey* conducted by the District School Board in Toronto, Canada's most cosmopolitan city. It found that 42 per cent of all secondary school students were born abroad and fewer than seven per cent of these new Canadians originated from European nations. In addition, less than half the students in Toronto speak either English or French as their mother tongue (Reed and Novogrodsky, 2000).

The initial response to the educational demands that the new diversity presented was a policy of multicultural education, adopted nationwide in 1971. However, its perceived failure to account for and respond to the relatively poor educational achievements of visible minority students led to the development of antiracist theory which takes the reality of racism and the disparity of educational outcomes as its starting point. Antiracist education appears to have had a significant impact in many parts of Canada (Bonnett and Carrington, 1996). Certainly, from the mid-1980s to the mid-1990s, the antiracist analysis of the under-achievement of visible minority children held much currency in Canadian education circles. For example, in Ontario from 1991 to 1996, under the influence of the left-leaning National Democratic Party (NDP), antiracism became the official model of 'race relations' and, as a public declaration of its commitment, the NDP renamed the provincial race relations division the Anti-Racist Directorate. It was also under this government that the provincial Ministry of Education issued a directive requiring every school board in the province to create its own antiracist education policy. However, the NDP was defeated in the election of 1996 and the right-wing Progressive Conservative government that succeeded it retracted the directive. It also effectively thwarted the growing influence of antiracism by removing financial support from many antiracist initiatives and by closing down the Anti-Racist Directorate.

Regardless of fluctuations in their level of influence, Canadian antiracists, like their British counterparts, have generally shown little interest in how the Holocaust is taught in schools. We believe this to be no mere oversight, for during the ascendancy of antiracist thought in Canada, there was a relatively high level of Holocaust awareness in the country. Books on the subject were numerous and widely available and Holocaust study was referenced in the secondary school history curricula in a number of provinces (including Ontario, New Brunswick and

British Columbia). For these reasons it is implausible to claim that the avoidance of Holocaust issues by antiracists has been nothing more than benign neglect. On the contrary, the failure of antiracists to embrace Holocaust education has resulted from, and has exacerbated, an unfortunate acrimony between the two projects.

To understand the attitude of Canadian antiracists to the Holocaust, we need to explain not indifference - the problem in the United Kingdom - but hostility; and to account for the latter, it is necessary to address an issue that has assumed considerable importance in the Canadian context. We refer to ideological divisions within the antiracist movement and specifically to the distinction between broad and narrow antiracism (Reed, 1994). The former (associated with Troyna and Williams, 1986 and Cohen, 1989) relies on the concept of racialisation, a process whereby one group of people sets apart another for unequal treatment using certain characteristics as signifiers for that treatment. Signifiers that function to racialise groups are often physical, like skin colour and hair type, but religion and cultural behaviour have also been employed to target a range of groups at different times in the past. As a result, the history of racism has encompassed a multiplicity of groups. In contrast to this view of racism as a plastic political phenomenon, narrow antiracists (such as Brandt, 1986 and Mullard, 1980) take a more exclusive view of the concept of 'race' and the parameters of the history of racism. They see the latter as the history of the oppression of people of colour. In the gap between these two schools of antiracist thought has arisen much confusion about the place of anti-Semitism in antiracist theory. To those committed to narrow antiracism, the inclusion of anti-Semitism is problematic, for they treat it not as a manifestation of racism but as a kind of ethnic prejudice. For them, the struggle against anti-Semitism and thus the study of the Holocaust is not properly a part of the antiracist agenda.

Over the years, the impact of narrow antiracism on Canadian academic thought has been considerably strengthened by the influence of American race and ethnic relations. In Canada, the concept of 'race' as defined by narrow antiracists has a powerful resonance due to the adopted 'memory' of American slavery and to the still deeply divisive race relations that continue to reverberate. Added to this is the sometimes fractious relationship between African-Americans and Jews (D'Souza, 1995) which spills over into Canadian ethnic relations. Further evidence of the American influence can be seen in the Afrocentric movement which has made major inroads into antiracist thought in Canada (Dei, 1993). It emphasises the importance of African identity and lends weight to the conceptualisation of 'race' as primarily an issue of skin colour predicated on the history of plantocratic slavery.

To comprehend the soured relationship between antiracism and the Holocaust we also need to bear in mind the effects of the Israeli-Palestinian conflict. In Canada, as in the United Kingdom, there has been much sympathy in left-wing circles over many years for the Palestinian cause and an undercurrent of animosity towards Israel. These factors conflate to form an unstated but keenly felt consensus among Canadian antiracists that for them to include anti-Semitism in their remit is not only inappropriate but counter-productive to their interests. In so far as the Holocaust is seen as a Jewish tragedy it is thus no more likely than anti-Semitism to be considered a legitimate concern for antiracists. They see it not as a potentially powerful antidote to the false promise of racist ideology, nor as an apt case study for antiracist education, but as an emotionally and politically charged subject that threatens to undermine the hegemonic position of what we have defined as narrowly focused antiracism.

Teaching the Holocaust to Ethnic Minorities: Outcomes and Possibilities

A major concern stemming from the antiracist rejection of anti-Semitism is that classroom practitioners may be hesitant to teach about the Holocaust as part of an antiracist initiative. It was in order to test this hypothesis that Reed and Novogrodsky (2000) recently carried out a small-scale survey of teachers who had participated in a course on Holocaust education. The researchers administered a questionnaire and conducted in-depth interviews with twelve teachers, seven of whom worked in secondary schools (Grades 9-13) and five in middle schools (Grades 6-8). Nearly all of them taught in the public system, but one was based in a Roman Catholic school and another worked in the independent sector. The classes of nine of the twelve teachers reflected the ethno-cultural diversity of the city; one teacher's students, for example, included immigrants from Poland, India, Greece, the Caribbean, China, Korea and Vietnam.

Many of the teachers, and especially those who were Jewish, reported feeling uneasy when dealing with the Holocaust. In particular, they feared that their visible minority students might object to spending time away from the issue of racism as defined by colour. They were very aware of the tensions between antiracism and Holocaust education and did not want to be seen as privileging the struggle against anti-Semitism over that of colour prejudice. Despite their initial apprehension, the majority did choose to teach about the Holocaust and found that their students rapidly became engaged with the lessons. Far from making theoretical distinctions between prejudice aimed at Jews on the one hand and at visible minorities on the other, the students made links between the two struggles. One teacher reported that his Korean and Vietnamese students were very quick to establish connections between anti-Semitism and the anti-Asian hostility they had encountered in Canada. He also reported that his openly gay students expressed a particular interest in this learning unit. Another wrote that a few of her Muslim students were a little reluctant at first to start the unit but almost immediately became 'interested and enthralled by the new knowledge.' In general, teachers experienced very little resistance from visible minority students who, as noted, tended to eschew the abstract distinctions between different kinds of discrimination that academics make. Reed and Novogrodsky suggest that 'perhaps these distinctions matter to academics and social scientists and do not matter much to the rich diversity of students living, studying and trying to get along together despite their varied backgrounds' (Reed and Novogrodsky, 2000:517).

Anecdotal evidence that the debates and theoretical tensions which are germane to academics are easily resolved in the daily practice of educators and students comes from the testimony of Holocaust survivors. In Ontario they share their experiences with students in classrooms and at the Holocaust Education and Memorial Centre in Toronto and those we have spoken to, without exception, are adamant that they make connections and not distinctions between different forms of racism. Survivors tell us that students from all kinds of background eagerly respond to their Holocaust narratives and frequently report warm embraces from Muslim and African-Caribbean students. (For evidence of a similar reaction in the United Kingdom, see Gill, 2004). Consistently, students thank them for recounting their stories and often share with the survivor their own personal accounts of pain resulting from discrimination. Clearly, these student reactions suggest that the theoretical impasse between antiracism and Holocaust education that some academics cannot, or will not, break through, does not have much currency with the students themselves.

Chapter 4

Curricular, Organisational and Ethical Issues

In this chapter we focus on some of the curricular, organisational and ethical issues pertinent to teaching the Holocaust. In relation to the formal curriculum, we consider a number of topics that, *prima facie*, might be deemed peripheral, but which actually have a crucial bearing on how both the Holocaust and its contemporary relevance are to be understood. The organisational issues we address relate to the hidden curriculum and specifically to the importance of establishing a school ethos conducive to promoting a caring community and reinforcing a commitment among students to democratic values. We conclude with a discussion of the ethical dimension of Holocaust education, drawing attention to some of the potential dangers inherent in teaching the subject such as giving credence to anti-Semitic stereotypes.

The first part of the chapter deals primarily with curricular content and the second with school organisation and ethical matters. However, as some of the issues we raise fall into more than one category, the chapter divisions are somewhat arbitrary.

CURRICULAR CONTENT

Other Victims; Other Genocides

While opinions may differ as to how the Holocaust should be defined, it is vital, as we have stated, that students are not left with the impression that the Jews were Hitler's only victims. Students should know that between 5,000 and 10,000 homosexuals were murdered in concentration camps and that at least a quarter of a million Roma and Sinti, nearly 2,000 Jehovah's Witnesses and as many as a quarter of a million Germans with disabilities were likewise 'eliminated.' In addition, students should be informed of the Nazi attitude towards the Slavs and of the cruelties that they endured and they should be taught too about the murder of tens of thousands of political dissidents within Nazi Germany and of millions of

Soviet prisoners of war. However, students must not be led to believe that the Nazis had identical attitudes towards their various victim groups and dealt them all the same fate. In her trenchant critique of Holocaust education in the United States, Lucy Dawidowicz (1992) was clearly angered by curricula that violated this imperative by enlarging 'the list of victims of Nazi genocide to include those whom the Nazis never intended to wipe out' (p. 76). Although there should be no attempt to minimise the suffering of any victim group, students ought to be aware of how the Nazis differentiated between them. For example, they should be conscious of the fact that whereas Jehovah's Witnesses could end their incarceration by renouncing their faith (a right, incidentally, that very few chose to exercise), religious Jews had no such option. They should also be aware of differences in Nazi policy towards Jews and the Roma and Sinti. As Guenter Lewy (1999) has observed:

> The Nazis never formulated a plan for a "Final Solution" to the Gypsy problem analogous to that for the Jews. ... Numerous sources, especially recently discovered local police files, show that large numbers of "racially pure" and "socially adjusted" Gypsies were exempted from deportation to the Gypsy family camp in Auschwitz and were allowed to survive the war.
>
> (Lewy, 1999:383)

Yehuda Bauer (1978) has also commented on the differential treatment of Jews and Roma and Sinti. Writing about the latter he notes that:

> those living among the rest of the population were not ferreted out and many even served in the Nazi army ... the Nazis were ambivalent about what to do with them, but those who were murdered were the victims more of a campaign against so-called 'a socials' than against the Gypsy people as such.
>
> (Bauer, 1978:36)

While it is important to make clear that Jews were the only group singled out by the Nazis for total annihilation, it is equally important to stress that in the course of human history, Jews have not been the only victims of genocide. To this end, reference ought to be made to other instances of mass slaughter that would include the indigenous peoples in many parts of the world, the Armenian genocide, the fate of the Kulaks under Stalin, the relatively recent atrocities in the former Yugoslavia and the 1994 genocide in Rwanda. But in the same way that students should realise that the Nazis' victims were not all treated alike, so they should know that genocides differ - not in terms of the suffering of the victims, but in terms of the motivation and intentions of the perpetrators. In the words of Deborah Lipstadt (1995):

> (To say that other tragedies are different from the Holocaust) is not a matter of comparative pain - an utterly useless exercise - but of historical distinction. The

issue is not who lost more people or a greater proportion of their society, but what was at the root of the genocidal efforts.

(Lipstadt, 1995:27)

The History of Anti-Semitism

In addition to addressing the history of genocide and the distinctive character of the Holocaust, it is essential that teachers spend some time discussing the history of anti-Semitism in order that the Holocaust be seen in perspective. It is of cardinal importance that in the course of their learning, students are not persuaded to conceive of Germans as peculiarly vulnerable to anti-Semitism. They ought, therefore, to be made aware that in Europe, anti-Semitism stretches back to Roman times; that during the Middle Ages Jews were accused, across the continent, of poisoning wells and of utilizing the blood of Christian children to bake Passover *matzot* and that Jews were expelled from many European countries beginning with England in 1290. Mention should be made of the Chelmenicki massacres in the Ukraine in the middle of the seventeenth century, the pogroms in Poland and Russia in the late nineteenth and early twentieth centuries as well as the Dreyfus affair in France. It should also be acknowledged, following the recent revelations by Jan Tomasz Gross (2001), that many Polish Jews were killed during the Second World War not by Germans, but by their fellow Poles. More generally, students should learn something of the nature of nationalism and of the potentially precarious position of *any* ethno-cultural group that is not regarded as legitimately belonging to the nation. In the nineteenth century, Jewish insecurities were heightened throughout much of Europe, and not just in Germany, as a result of the growth of nationalist ideology.

Equally important is that students are informed of the historic role played by the Church in promoting the image of the Jew as Christ-killer and as the Devil incarnate and that they appreciate the cumulative effects of such imagery in creating a climate receptive to anti-Semitic rhetoric and propaganda. As former Archbishop of Canterbury, Robert Runcie, made clear on the fiftieth anniversary of the *Kristallnacht* pogrom, 'Without the poisoning of Christian minds through the centuries, the Holocaust is unthinkable' (cited in Braybrooke, 1993:69). To reinforce further the notion of the Holocaust as, in part, the product of centuries of Christian teachings, it might prove instructive for teachers to focus briefly on Martin Luther's *On the Jews and their Lies* published in 1543. Dagmar Lorenz (1996:59) points out that the book 'reads like a blueprint for the Nazi *Judenprogramm*' and there are, indeed, a number of parallels. For example, the burning of synagogues and Jewish books in Nazi Germany was one of Luther's recommendations, as was another feature of Nazi Germany, the imposition on Jews of travel and residential restrictions. It should further be noted that apart from the

Jews, the only group that Luther referred to as a threat to his fellow Germans was the Gypsies.

In dealing with the role of the Church, mention must, of course, be made of the Vatican and its relationship with the Nazis. Students should know not only about the Concordat of 1933, but of the persistent refusal of Pius XII to speak out publicly against the Nazis' anti-Semitic policies even when, in the autumn of 1943, the Jews of Rome were being deported. They should not, however, assume that Vatican policy was entirely unambiguous; nor that all Catholic clergy were unsympathetic to Jews. They should know that the majority of the Jews of Rome were hidden in the city's convents and monasteries and they should be aware of the explicit condemnation of the Holocaust by the Dutch bishops in 1942 and of the rescue activities of Papal Nuncios in Slovakia, Hungary, Romania and Turkey. [For a comprehensive and balanced overview of the role of the Catholic and Protestant churches during the Holocaust, see Rittner *et al.*, 2000.]

Responsibility for the Holocaust: Attributing Blame

We have just referred to the need to protect students from the slander that anti-Semitism has a significantly stronger appeal for Germans than it has for many other nationalities. No less necessary is the need to protect them from the equally baseless charge that all Germans bear responsibility for the Holocaust. It is important to engage with both accusations, not only because it would be deeply ironic for students to acquire an unfounded prejudice as a result of learning about the Holocaust,[†] but because ample evidence exists to refute each of the charges. As far as the second is concerned, students must be helped to distinguish between Germans and Nazis. They should be alerted to the extent of political opposition to the far-right prior to Hitler's accession to power and they should know that even in the election of March 1933, two months after he became Chancellor, more than half the electorate voted against the Nazi party despite the use of propaganda and widespread intimidation. Students should also be aware of (the admittedly few) individual acts of defiance towards the regime. Apart from clerics such as Bernhard Lichtenberg and Dietrich Bonhoeffer and the more contentious case of Martin Niemöller, mention ought to be made of the 'White Rose' movement established in 1942 by Hans and Sophie Scholl, the only German group that spoke out publicly against their country's genocidal policies.

To undermine further the association of anti-Semitism with Germany alone, reference should be made to the collaborators found in every country the Germans

---

[†] Some German educationalists and politicians have recently suggested that British children acquire negative feelings towards Germans as a result of learning only about the Nazi era in German history (*The Times*, October 9, 2003).

occupied (including the British Channel Islands) and to the existence, in a number of European countries, of indigenous Fascist and anti-Semitic movements such as the Iron Guard in Romania and the Arrow Cross in Hungary. Moreover, students ought to know that Hitler, other high-ranking Nazis and prominent career bureaucrats such as Eichmann, were Austrian by birth, as were two-thirds of the death camp commandants. Outside of Europe, students should learn that anti-Semitism was not only prevalent, but played a major part in blocking the emigration of German and Austrian Jews in the 1930s. In the United States, for example, as David Wyman (1996b) points out, between 1880 and 1930 'racial anti-Semitism became an important factor in the move to close America's doors to large-scale immigration.' He goes on to claim that:

> By the mid-1930s, quotas were prevalent throughout the nation's private colleges and medical schools. Jews were also excluded from some residential areas. They were discriminated against in much of the business world, from the secretarial and clerical levels to the top, as was openly displayed in employment advertisements in newspapers.
>
> (Wyman, 1996b:696)

Many other examples of American anti-Semitism during this period could be cited. Best known, perhaps, is the case of Father Charles Coughlin of Detroit whose anti-Semitic diatribes were broadcast weekly on American radio and syndicated across the country to an estimated audience of around fourteen million. There was also the Mothers Movement, a confederation of far-right women's groups that, according to Glen Jeansonne (1999:31), 'combined maternal rhetoric and anti-Semitism, love of Jesus and hatred of President Roosevelt.' Among other things, it campaigned against the admission of Jewish refugees into the United States.

Irving Abella and Frank Bialystok (1996) make clear that the situation facing Jews in Canada at this time was no more congenial. They recount one notorious event.

> In June 1934 occurred one of the most bizarre strikes in Canadian history ... Samuel Rabinovitch, a young medical student who had graduated first in his class at the University of Montreal, was offered an internship at Notre Dame Hospital. On the day he was to begin work all fourteen of his fellow interns walked out, refusing, as they put it, to work with a Jew. They picketed the hospital and refused to accept even emergency cases, their newly sworn Hippocratic oath not withstanding. They were soon joined by fellow interns from five surrounding Catholic hospitals, as well as by the clergy of neighbouring parishes.
>
> It was a sensational story, and the French-language press gave it front-page coverage. The interns were all interviewed and their story told sympathetically. None wished to spend a full year working with a Jew - who could blame them, asked Quebec's leading French-language newspaper, Le Devoir - and all were concerned that Catholic patients would find it 'repugnant' to be treated, or even touched, by a Jewish physician. To the support of the indignant interns came such organizations as the Jean Baptiste Society, the Association of Young Catholics,

various county councils and cooperatives, as well as prominent members of the Catholic clergy. Within a few days Rabinovitch submitted his resignation, and the hospital promised never to hire any Jewish doctors. Jews, a Quebec paper gloated, have now learned their place, and 'it is not in Quebec.'

(Abella and Bialystok, 1996:749)

As Abella and Bialystok go on to remind us, 'the *grève internes* was one of literally hundreds of anti-Semitic incidents that marked Canadian society in the years between the wars' (*ibid.*).

In considering the degree of culpability of the Allies and neutral states for the Holocaust, students' attention should be drawn to two further matters. The first is the Evian conference held in France in July 1938. It was convened by President Roosevelt to deal with the mounting refugee problem but, for the most part, representatives of the countries attending revealed only their callous indifference to the plight of German and Austrian Jews. By way of illustration, the Canadian delegate was told by his prime minister 'to listen, make notes and say as little as possible' (Abella and Bialystok, *ibid.*, 756). Similar sentiments were voiced by others, such as the Australian delegate who stated that his country had no racial problem and no desire to import one. To strengthen students' sense of the heartlessness of much of the international community at this time, they ought to be acquainted with the fate of the refugees on board the *St. Louis* which, in the summer of 1939, was refused landing rights by Cuba, the United States and Canada and, as a result, was forced to return to Europe with disastrous consequences for most of those on board.

The other matter relating to the responsibility of the Allied and neutral nations concerns the controversy over the failure to bomb the death camps. While students should be told that the western powers knew of the fate of European Jewry from mid-1942, they should, at the same time, be apprised of the reasons for not bombing.

Rescue and Resistance

Although the number of rescuers in Nazi-occupied Europe was pitifully small, their heroism and in some cases their self-sacrifice must be acknowledged, not just to satisfy the demands of historical truth, but in the hope of influencing the behaviour of students. With this aim in mind, rescuers should be celebrated and seen as role models, the latter requiring that teachers focus rather more on those who were ordinary members of the public than on their better known counterparts in positions of relative power. This is not to suggest that teachers overlook or minimise the efforts of diplomats such as Raoul Wallenberg, Aristedes de Sousa Mendes and Ho Fengshan - far from it. We simply wish to emphasise that students will find it easier to identify with rescuers who can be seen as similar to themselves in terms of influence and status. For this reason reference should be made not only to named individuals, but to the Danish fishermen who, in 1943, ferried almost all of their country's Jewish population to safety in Sweden and to the Protestant villagers of Le Chambon-sur-Lignon in south-central France who, it is believed, sheltered between 3,000 and 5,000 Jews during the course of the war.

Jewish resistance, limited though it was, must also be acknowledged. Countering the myth that all Jews went to their deaths like lambs to the slaughter not only sets the historical record straight, but makes it more likely that students will empathise with the victims; for passivity in the face of the oppressor (no matter how understandable) may be seen as a trait more deserving of contempt than compassion. Students should therefore learn about the uprising in Warsaw and in the other ghettos of eastern Europe and they should learn too about the revolts that resulted in the closure of the Sobibor and Treblinka death camps. No less important, of course, is that they are made aware of the awesome nature of the obstacles to armed resistance, especially the use by the Nazis of collective punishment. In the Bialystok ghetto, for example, the Germans murdered 120 Jews in 1943 as a reprisal for the shooting of a single German policeman (Gilbert, 1986). Although some historians, notably Raul Hilberg (1985), see resistance only in terms of armed actions of this kind, others offer a broader definition. Among them is Yehuda Bauer (1980:27) who argues that resistance should be regarded as 'any group action consciously taken in opposition to known or surmised laws, actions or intentions directed against the Jews by the Germans or their supporters.' Clearly, the observance of religious laws, including the celebration of festivals, is encompassed by this definition and should, in our view, be taught as an aspect of Jewish resistance. So should the writing of poetry, the keeping of journals and the creation of works of art in the ghettos and camps, for they were often undertaken in the hope of holding the victimisers accountable. The same camps and ghettos frequently witnessed acts of solidarity and kindness and they too should be seen as legitimate forms of resistance, for they were performed in violation of permitted behaviour and thus at great personal risk.

Perceptions of Jews and Judaism

One other issue relating to content that teachers need to take into account is the knowledge of Jews that students possess before they formally encounter the Holocaust. The importance of uncovering this knowledge, and engaging with it if necessary, is self-evident, for students will not automatically recoil in horror as a result of discovering the full extent of the Nazi persecution of the Jews. How they react will depend, in large part, on how they regard Jews, and if they see them as in some sense 'bad people,' their response to learning of their fate may be less one of revulsion than of joy at the perceived triumph of good over evil. In addition, any misunderstanding that students have of Judaism could lead them to conceptualise Jews as an alien group having little in common with themselves and this may, in turn, affect their reaction to the Holocaust, making it that much more difficult for them to identify with the victims. In order to offer teachers of the Holocaust some insight into how young adolescents are likely to construe Jews and Judaism, we summarise below the principal findings of a study carried out in south-east England just over a decade ago (Short, 1994a). The sample, comprising 35 boys and 37 girls aged between 12 and 14, was drawn from two predominantly white and 'Christian' comprehensive schools. All the students had spent some time during the previous two years examining aspects of Judaism.

One of the assumptions underpinning the research was that Christian (or nominally Christian) students would be more inclined to hold Nazism in contempt the more they saw Judaism having in common with Christianity. This reasoning lay behind the following questions: (1) Do Jews and Christians worship the same God? (2) What was Jesus' religion? and (3) How did Jesus die?

More than 40 per cent of the students believed that Jews and Christians worship different gods. Some said that Jews pray to Allah, while others were sure that Jews and Christians prayed to different deities, although they could not name the Jewish one. A few claimed that the two religions did venerate the same god, but that Jews also revered their own. With regard to the questions on Jesus, it was found that more than a third of the students either thought he was a Christian or did not know his religious identity; most, however, were aware that he was a Jew. Roughly two-thirds accused the Romans of killing him and just a handful held the Jews responsible, but the fact that there were any at all has to be a matter of concern to Holocaust educators. Also of concern were those who were unsure of the circumstances surrounding his death for their ignorance renders them vulnerable to the traditional account of the Passion stressing Jewish guilt.

To test the students' familiarity with anti-Semitic stereotypes, they were asked if they had ever heard anything 'nasty or unkind' said about Jews. [So as not to give credence to any lingering suspicion that Jews are more likely to be spoken about disparagingly than any other group, the students were first asked whether they had heard anything similarly unflattering about Christians.] The vast majority had encountered negative comments, often in the form of references to the common stereotypes of avarice and parsimony, but none of those who were questioned directly, or who commented spontaneously, said that they accepted the truth content of the stereotypes. In contrast, some students did subscribe to outlandish notions of Judaism. The following statements, made in response to the question, 'What do you know about Judaism?' are representative and, in the first two cases, reflected a recent project on Passover.

> They have to put those things outside their door.
> *Interviewer:* What's that?
> They put blood.

We know about the Passover ... that they have to put blood on their doors, otherwise the oldest child of the family - the Jewish family - will die.

Is it a religion where you have to put dye all over your face?

It is difficult to imagine the origin of some of the students' beliefs about Judaism, although in the first of the statements given below, the content might suggest an anti-Semitic influence.

When someone dies and you go to their door asking for money, they have to give you some money.

When they get buried they have to be stood up.

If students are to understand the essence of the Holocaust they will need to know how the Nazis defined Jewish identity. To be precise, they will need to be *au fait* with the concept of consanguinity. They were therefore asked whether someone born Jewish who converted to Christianity 'would stop being Jewish completely.' The overwhelming majority thought that converts would remain Jewish in some sense, but very few referred to 'blood ties' as the reason. Most said that converts would remain Jewish either because they would be unable to shake off the effects of their upbringing, or because there was no incompatibility between the two faiths and thus no difficulty in practising both. These responses emphasise the need for teachers, when dealing with the Holocaust, to make clear to students that Jewish identity in Nazi ideology was 'racial' rather than religious and that the Jews who perished in the Holocaust were not by definition committed to Judaism. To illustrate the point, students might learn about Edith Stein, the Jewish woman who not only converted to Catholicism but became a Carmelite nun. This did not, however, prevent her deportation to Auschwitz where, in 1942, she was murdered.

Before leaving the subject of students' perceptions of Jews and Judaism, it should be noted that when discussing stereotypes, there was no reference to the Jew as invariably wealthy. Had the question dealing with stereotypes been phrased differently such references may well have emerged, for the association of Jews with opulence is widespread in western societies and is certainly known to primary school children (Short, 1991a). It is an association that is problematic for Holocaust educators not just because it is a misleading generalisation, but because it may function to deflect students' sympathies away from the victims. Students should know that Jews have been persecuted throughout the ages regardless of their economic status, but a reliance on facts of any kind to undermine a stereotype so deeply embedded in a culture may be unwise. Teachers should therefore go beyond the facts and engage their pupils in a discussion of the morality of wealth. The aim of such discussion would be twofold. First, to encourage a recognition that the critical moral issue in relation to wealth is not its possession, but the means by which it is acquired; and second, to foster an awareness that the operation of a double standard whereby it is acceptable to persecute the rich if they are Jews, but not otherwise, cannot be justified under any circumstances.

PEDAGOGIC AND ETHICAL ISSUES

School Ethos

The chief organisational issue we believe it necessary to address is that of school ethos, a characteristic of the educational system that has long been acknowledged as crucial to the promotion of citizenship and the teaching of democracy. Nearly a hundred years ago the philosopher and educator John Dewey (1916) was insistent that teachers could not adequately prepare their students for democracy just by transmitting a body of knowledge; schools also had to be run democratically and this meant, amongst other things, limiting authoritarian relationships within them. Throughout the twentieth century similar sentiments were echoed by academics in the field of human rights education including those involved with 'race' and ethnicity. Gordon Allport (1954) was a prominent enthusiast.

> As in the home, the atmosphere that surrounds the child at school is exceedingly important. If segregation of the sexes or races prevails, if authoritarianism and hierarchy dominate the system, the child cannot help but learn that power and status are the dominant factors in human relationships. If, on the other hand, the school system is democratic, if the teacher and child are each respected units, the lesson of respect for the person will easily register. As in society at large, the *structure* of the pedagogic system will blanket, and may negate, the specific intercultural lessons taught.
>
> (Allport, 1954:511. Original emphasis)

In the United Kingdom, the importance of the relationship between the way a school is run and the learning that takes place within it, was recognised and highlighted in the final report of the Advisory Group on Citizenship (DfEE, 1998). It stated that 'schools need to consider to what extent their ethos, organisation and daily practices are consistent with the aim and purpose of citizenship education, and provide opportunities for pupils to develop into active citizens' (p. 55). While this exhortation is to be welcomed, it must be admitted that with few exceptions (such as Summerhill and Dartington Hall in England) schools have never operated as democratic institutions and there are clear limits to the extent to which they can be made more democratic. However, Alf Davey (1983), who shares Allport's concern that the medium be compatible with the message, suggests how the two might be brought closer together. Although commenting on multicultural education, his remarks are equally pertinent to teaching about the Holocaust.

> Purging the textbooks of black stereotypes, boosting the minority groups in the teaching materials and adjusting the curriculum to accommodate cultural diversity, will have little impact on how children treat each other, if teachers make rules without explanation, if they command needlessly and assume their authority to be established by convention. We learn to cooperate with one another, not by hearing about cooperation, or by reading about cooperation, or even by discussing cooperation, but by living in a community in which cooperation is practised and rewarded. ... (Teachers) need frequently to re-examine whether the way in which they group children together for different purposes, the manner in which they negotiate with them and the extent to which they are prepared to share their authority with them, is likely to foster or inhibit intergroup friendship.
>
> (Davey, 1983:181-182)

Arguably, the Holocaust educator best known for stressing the importance of school ethos is the American academic Pearl Oliner (1986). She maintains that:

> It is out of a sense of community that people are more likely to engage in those acts of kindness, civility and helpfulness which enhance the quality of life. It is in the context of community consciousness that individuals begin to feel expansive responsibilities towards each other.
>
> (Oliner, 1986:397)

She goes on to plead for schools to be transformed into more caring communities where:

> Students, teachers, bus drivers, principals, and all others receive positive affirmation for kindness, empathy and concern ... What is required is nothing less than institutionalised structures that promote supportive relationships with the same seriousness as is currently devoted to academic achievement.
>
> (Oliner and Oliner, 1988:258/259)

She recognises that in order to facilitate such a transformation it will be necessary, among other things, to re-structure the nature of citizenship education. The approach she derides concentrates on the institutions of government, dealing with topics such as political parties, elections and constitutional issues and with key political concepts such as democracy. Oliner believes that this emphasis on government is excessive and she decries the absence in social studies programmes of any reference to prosocial citizenship behaviours that 'demonstrate caring and concern and ... increase feelings of benevolence, bonding and rootedness' (*ibid.*).

Promoting Anti-Semitism

A major ethical concern inherent in teaching about the Holocaust is the risk of unintentionally fostering anti-Semitism. It will be recalled from Chapter 1 that Lionel Kochan is opposed to schools teaching about the fate of European Jewry during the Second World War partly because it reinforces the stereotype of the Jew as 'predestined victim of persecution.' However, the problem, in our view, goes beyond the reproduction of unflattering imagery, for subject matter that reinforces the widespread association of Jewish history with persecution could prompt some students to assume that there is no smoke without fire and to conclude that Jews are, at least to some extent, the authors of their own misfortune. There has long been a school of thought that sees Jews in this light, a form of blaming the victim that Brian Cheyette (1990) refers to as the 'interactionist model of racial hatred.' Among the more illustrious names associated with it is that of the British novelist and Liberal Member of Parliament Hilaire Belloc and the writer H. G. Wells. In his book, *The Jews*, published in 1922, Belloc claimed that 'the anti-Semitic movement is essentially a reaction against the abnormal growth in Jewish power and the new strength of anti-Semitism is largely due to the Jews themselves' (p. 159). In the same vein, Wells wrote that 'There is room for some very serious research into the question why anti-Semitism emerges in every country the Jews reside in' (cited in Wheatcroft, 1996:340). While noting that this line of thought continues to find an echo in certain quarters (surfacing most recently in the David Irving libel trial) there are 'reasons' other than so-called 'Jewish behaviour' why some might accept that Jews should be held responsible for anti-Semitism. In particular, in societies where the Christian motif of the Jew as Christ-killer is deeply ingrained in popular consciousness, students may be more inclined to indulge a religious version of the interactionist model and interpret the Holocaust as the ultimate act of expiation.

It is clearly unacceptable to teach history in such a way as to strengthen the suspicion that an entire ethnic or religious group is eternally damned. This is not just because such teaching threatens the most fundamental tenet of natural justice, namely, that the innocent should not suffer along with the guilty, but because, in the case of the Jews, it is simply bad history. As we have already indicated, the Jewish past is not synonymous with unremitting torment and should not be taught as though it was.

A second way in which teaching about the Holocaust could give rise to anti-Semitism stems from having to acquaint students with anti-Semitic propaganda, for they will need to know how the Nazis conceptualised Jews in order to understand why the genocide was planned and implemented. Some students will be learning about anti-Semitic stereotypes for the first time; others will already be familiar with them as a result of what they have gleaned from parents and peers or come across in the media. The moral imperative for teachers is to ensure that they do nothing to reinforce these beliefs and whatever they can to undermine them. This objective, however, is unlikely to be realised; indeed, the opposite may be the case if students are merely *told about* the existence and content of anti-Semitic stereotypes. The problem here is twofold. On the one hand there can be no doubt that Germany, at the time of the Nazi take-over, was in many respects a culturally sophisticated society and was indisputably a technologically advanced one. A substantial number of influential and well-educated people subscribed to anti-Semitic stereotypes, and if this fact is made known to students, as it should be, along with all other relevant facts, the stereotypes may well acquire an enhanced status by association. They may be seen to possess a core of respectability that would be denied them had they been accepted and articulated exclusively by the disaffected, the uneducated and the socially disadvantaged. The second problem with merely informing students of the content of Jewish stereotypes central to Nazi philosophy is that the media (wittingly or otherwise) occasionally reinforce them and thus, once again, add to their credibility. A relatively recent example involved attempts by Holocaust survivors across the world to recover assets that before the war had been lodged in Swiss bank accounts. The publicity surrounding the attempt to return the contents of these deposits to their original owners may well have reinforced the perception of Jews as invariably affluent; it certainly did nothing to weaken the association in the popular imagination of Jews with money. Another example that occurred some years earlier concerned George Soros, by all accounts an exceptionally wealthy Jewish financier who, at the time of the United Kingdom's forced departure from the Exchange Rate Mechanism, was described in the Press as a Hungarian born Jew and as 'the man said to have broken the pound' (*The Times*, December 19, 1992). If students learn from studying Nazi propaganda that Jews are an unpatriotic element intent on manipulating both the domestic and the international economy for their own ends, such portrayals may be seen to legitimate Nazi claims and, in the process, help to engender sympathy for the perpetrators of the Final Solution rather than its victims. In order to avoid such an outcome it will be necessary to expose students to the fraudulent nature of anti-Semitic beliefs and, more generally, to teach them about the nature of stereotyping. Ideally, this type of work would be undertaken as part of an antiracist or moral education programme carried out some time prior to studying the Holocaust. Research suggests that initiatives of this kind can be pursued successfully in the upper reaches of the primary school (Short and Carrington, 1991).

One further way in which teaching about the Holocaust could lead to a growth in anti-Semitism arises from the Nazi perception of the Jews as a racial group rather than a religious one. Students who are not conversant with this crucial distinction will need to made aware of it, but in so doing, is there not a risk of teachers encouraging their pupils to regard Jews as an alien wedge, a nation within a nation and thus potentially as the enemy within? No means of countering such a perception can be sanctioned if it involves distorting the truth and thus students should not be led to believe that the Jews perished because of their religious convictions. A more ethical and certainly an educationally more useful means of dealing with this problem would seem to require that at an early stage in their learning about the Holocaust, students consider whether there are any grounds on which it is legitimate to cause suffering to an *entire* racial or ethnic group rather than to individual members of that group. The intention of such an exercise would be to bring students to a realisation that people ought only to suffer as a result of human agency if they have committed an unjust act, and that belonging to an ethnic, racial or religious group by accident of birth cannot possibly be construed as constituting such an act.

Freedom of Speech

Another ethical considerations related to teaching about the Holocaust is the extent to which freedom of speech should be permitted in the classroom. It is manifestly not the case that everyone regards the attempted destruction of European Jewry as an unmitigated evil and in this sense the subject can be seen as controversial. Bearing in mind that even children of primary school age are capable of articulating anti-Semitic sentiments (Carrington and Short, 1993), the question that faces teachers of adolescents is whether, in the interests of freedom of speech, they ought to allow the expression of any view that would appear to justify, or even to condone, the Holocaust. If teachers are prepared to provide a platform for such views, they will need to consider whether they ought to respond and, if so, the form that their response should take. Over the past couple of decades, the issue of how to deal with controversial issues in the classroom has featured prominently in the debate over political education in schools. Doug Harwood (1986), who has made a significant contribution to this debate, lists the range of options available to teachers. While most demand that, at some stage, teachers make their views known to their pupils, others insist on them keeping their own counsel. Harwood's own preference is for what has come to be known as the neutral chairperson role or procedural neutrality. This position was initially proposed by Lawrence Stenhouse (1970) when directing the Humanities Curriculum Project and requires teachers to allow all sides of an argument to be heard while ensuring their own views remain firmly under wraps. However, as Robert Jeffcoate (1984), a keen supporter of neutrality, points out:

> This did not mean that teachers were to abrogate all their normal responsibilities. They were expected to aim for orderly and purposeful discussions, querying and challenging where necessary, restraining the voluble and encouraging the diffident, above all trying to get their pupils to submit to 'the discipline of the evidence'.
> (Jeffcoate, 1984:140)

The neutral chair approach has been seen to work well in respect of certain controversial issues, but for others, it has been widely condemned as inappropriate. Citing a study by Stradling *et al.* (1984), Singh (1988) argues that:

> (If) students have a lot to say, if there is a broad spread of opinion, and if their views are based on knowledge and experience, rather than blind prejudice, then there is a good case for adopting the role of a neutral chair. In other circumstances, the balanced or more committed approach might be more appropriate.
>
> (Singh, 1988:96)

There would seem to be particular dangers in employing the neutral chair in respect of the Holocaust. First, teachers' refusal to voice their own point of view might be construed by students, not as a pedagogic strategy designed to encourage open, coherent and rigorous enquiry, but rather as an inability to decide where truth and justice lie with regard to Nazi racial ideology. While equivocation might be acceptable and even desirable in an area of genuine historical debate, in relation to the Holocaust, it would be unconscionable. A further objection to neutrality is that some students might simply interpret their teacher's impartiality as indifference, leading them to conclude that the Holocaust is a topic of little consequence. Whatever the objection, the net result would be to diminish the significance of the Holocaust in the eyes of the students and for this reason, if for no other, the neutral chair must be rejected as a morally unacceptable basis for debate and discussion in this area of the curriculum. However, while teachers ought to state publicly their abhorrence of the Holocaust and the thinking that underpinned it, there should be no attempt to silence contrary opinion. The classroom atmosphere should be such that students feel free to state whatever beliefs they hold, for only if anti-Semitic attitudes and other manifestations of prejudice are openly articulated can they be effectively challenged.

Although we recognise that some teachers might hold anti-Semitic views, they cannot, of course, be granted the same freedom of expression that their pupils enjoy. On the contrary, any attempt to articulate pro-Nazi sympathies should, in our view, result in instant dismissal. Although there have been no cases of this kind in the United Kingdom, there have been a couple in Canada. We referred in Chapter 2 to the better known. It involved James Keegstra, a high-school history teacher in Alberta who was brought to trial in 1984. According to Joseph Kirman (1986):

> Keegstra was teaching children that there was a Jewish conspiracy to take over the world. The Jews were being blamed for communism and capitalism, and the Holocaust of World War II was being called a hoax.
>
> (Kirman, 1986:209)

After protracted legal wrangling, Keegstra was eventually fined 5,000 (Canadian) dollars. His case was followed by that of a New Brunswick teacher,

Malcolm Ross, who, in 1991, was barred from the classroom for writing books disputing the existence of the Holocaust.

Holocaust Denial

Perhaps the most troubling aspect of freedom of speech concerns the approach that ought to be adopted towards revisionist 'historians' who wish to deny or to trivialise the Holocaust. The question, though, is not just whether, in the interests of protecting the liberal ideal of reasoned dialogue, teachers should allow discussion of the revisionist point of view, but whether they should take the initiative and raise the issue if their pupils do not. Some writers are in no doubt that they should; Carlos Huerta and Dafna Shiffman-Huerta (1996) going so far as to advocate that students be encouraged to read revisionist literature of various kinds. However, it is not clear from their article whether they make this recommendation with both schoolchildren and university students in mind or with the latter group only.

The dilemma facing teachers is that if they encourage, or even permit, denial to be raised in the classroom they risk weakening, and maybe destroying, the Holocaust's status as a subject worthy of serious scholarship; for merely by making students aware of the revisionist point of view is to give it a degree of credibility. And when we acknowledge just how extraordinary a phenomenon the Holocaust was, denial has an intuitive plausibility. [Elie Wiesel (1983) Nobel Laureate and Holocaust survivor, has claimed that 'Auschwitz defies imagination and perception.'] But a deliberate decision to suppress all mention of revisionism is also problematic. In the first instance it might be thought to raise the spectre of indoctrination and in so far as only one side of the 'debate' is put forward, it could be argued that there is a *prima facie* case to answer. The charge, however, cannot be sustained, for one of the defining characteristics of indoctrination (deriving from its etymological connection with doctrine) is that it involves an attempt to inculcate beliefs the truth of which cannot rationally be demonstrated. On this ground alone, the wealth of documentary, photographic and eye-witness testimony puts paid to any suggestion of indoctrination. There is, though, a second and an entirely valid argument for teaching the revisionist point of view; namely, that a failure to do so would leave students unprepared to deal with the sophistry should they encounter it later in life. Subjecting Holocaust denial to critical scrutiny on the other hand, examining the grounds on which it casts doubt on the existence of the death camps, can help to inoculate students against the claim that all talk of a Holocaust is nothing more than a Zionist-inspired hoax. However, as we show in the following chapter, textbooks on the Holocaust that are in use in schools rarely adopt this position. A notable exception is Carrie Supple's (1993b) *From Prejudice to Genocide*. A couple of pages in the book are devoted to a discussion of revisionism and pupils are urged to reflect not only on the nature of historical evidence but on the motives some people have for ignoring or distorting it.

The Infliction of Pain

While the conditions under which one person may legitimately inflict pain on another may be a matter of opinion, the wilful infliction of pain without good reason can never be justified. Learning about the Holocaust, if it is taken seriously, will necessarily be an emotionally taxing experience for all but the psychologically deranged, yet there can be no doubt that the learning is intended to serve a valuable purpose. Summarising a number of the arguments we advanced in Chapter 1, Landau (1989) contends that:

> If taught properly the Holocaust can civilise and humanise our students and, perhaps more effectively than any other subject, has the power to sensitise them to the dangers of indifference, intolerance, racism and the dehumanisation of others - the ideal educational formula for creating good responsible citizens in a multicultural society.
>
> (Landau, 1989:20)

The moral issue concerns the lengths to which teachers are entitled to go in informing pupils of the horrors of the Holocaust. Downey and Kelly (1986:160) assert that, 'most of us respond to moral issues rather more often according to how we feel about them than as a result of a carefully thought-out intellectual appraisal.' If they are right, it follows that teachers ought to make a conscious effort to engage their pupils' emotions, but at what point ought they to call a halt? Clearly, it is unacceptable to subject students to any more pain than the minimum necessary to achieve the desired effect - a feeling of revulsion at where racism and anti-Semitism can lead, but in practice this will be a difficult judgment to make. The film *Warsaw Ghetto* was included as part of the original *Facing History and Ourselves* curriculum because of its vivid portrayal of the suffering of Polish Jews. However, Betty Bardige (1981) has observed that:

> Students at all levels, even though they are prepared for what they will see, respond with great emotion. Some cry, some feel like vomiting, some get angry. Some students need to discuss the film, others are unable to talk or write.
>
> (Bardige, 1981:44)

Similarly, Dawidowicz (1992:71) observed that role-play techniques designed to teach the moral lessons of the Holocaust 'have been known to produce unprecedented tension in the classroom ...' In view of these claims, the solution to the problem of how far to go may be to let individual students decide for themselves. When they feel they can take no more, they should literally be allowed to walk away until such time as they regain their composure and feel able to return to focus on some less painful aspect of the lesson.

While the ethical dimensions of inflicting pain has constantly to be borne in mind, teachers need also to take cognisance of the pedagogic implications of painful material. In other words, they must appreciate the relationship between anxiety and the ability to learn. To understand the connection, the literature on the psychology of persuasive communications while not, perhaps, directly analogous, is none the less instructive. In contrast to earlier research (e.g. Janis and Feshback, 1953), McGuire (1969) found that high rather than low levels of fear were effective in promoting attitude change. Very high levels of fear, however, engendered avoidance and defensiveness. The implications for teaching the Holocaust are self-evident.

There is one further issue that should be addressed when dealing with the question of pain. It concerns the way in which teachers ought to treat the presence within their classroom of students who identify themselves closely with any of the groups singled out by the Nazis for persecution. Their pain threshold may be significantly lower than that of other children, necessitating a special sensitivity on the part of teachers. The situation has close parallels with research in the area of children's racial attitudes where black youngsters have sometimes been subjected to an intolerably high degree of stress. The problem is well illustrated in the classic American study by Clark and Clark (1947). When their subjects, aged between 3 and 7, were presented with an array of dolls, some of which were black and others white and were then asked to make self-identifications, a number of the children 'who were free and relaxed at the beginning of the experiment, broke down and cried' (p. 611). It has been claimed that in the United Kingdom, partly as a result of such studies, 'those with a responsibility for authorising research in the area of children and 'race' are more alert to the possibility of (causing) distress and are consequently ... circumspect in their treatment of research proposals involving black children' (Short, 1994b:61). In contrast, there would seem to be no concern among educationalists, nor even any recognition, that learning about the Holocaust may be a qualitatively different experience for some students than it is for others. Whether the parents of students deemed to be particularly vulnerable to learning about the Holocaust should have the right to withdraw them from this part of the curriculum is a question worthy of consideration.

Chapter 5

Teachers' Attitudes and Practices

Thus far, we have concentrated on theoretical aspects of Holocaust education. We have looked at various reasons for teaching the subject and considered some of its curricular, organisational and ethical dimensions. We have also emphasised the contribution the subject can make to antiracism. In this chapter and the one that follows, the focus shifts from theory to practice in the sense that we attempt to find out what goes on in classrooms in the name of Holocaust education and endeavour to assess its effectiveness in promoting students' understanding of citizenship. We begin with two studies that examine the attitudes and practices of history staff in secondary schools. The first was conducted in England; the second in Ontario. (For a more detailed account of this research see Short, 1995, 1999, 2000b).

THE ATTITUDES AND PRACTICES OF TEACHERS IN ENGLAND

The study we describe extended the work of Supple (1992) and was carried out between October 1994 and July 1995. The sample comprised 34 history teachers, 30 of whom were Head of Department. They were drawn from 32 mixed-ability secondary schools chosen at random from five local education authorities in and around London. The vast majority of schools were multi-ethnic - in three cases predominantly so - and a few had a significant number of Jewish pupils.

A semi-structured interview schedule, the principal source of data collection, contained questions that fell into one of three categories: (1) Basic information (e.g. amount of time spent teaching the Holocaust), (2) Attitudes towards teaching the Holocaust and (3) Issues relating to content and pedagogy. The questions were as follows:

> Should schools teach about the Holocaust? What do you see as the main advantages and disadvantages of teaching the subject?
>
> How old are the students to whom you teach the Holocaust? Do you see any advantages or disadvantages in teaching it either to an older or younger age group?
>
> How much time do you spend on the Holocaust? Is this adequate? If not, what would you teach, or spend longer teaching, if time permitted?

What resources do you use?

Do you personally feel comfortable teaching about the Holocaust? If not, what are the sources of your discomfort: inadequate knowledge, deficiency in textbooks and other materials, nature of the subject matter, other?

Do you relate the Holocaust to contemporary developments - that is, the resurgence of nationalism and racism across much of Europe?

Do you draw parallels between the Holocaust and atrocities committed against other ethnic groups in the past?

How much time do you spend discussing the history of anti-Semitism in Europe and the role of the Church in perpetuating it?

Have you encountered students who have been traumatised as a result of learning about the Holocaust? If so, how did you handle such situations?

Would you alter your approach to teaching about the Holocaust depending on the ethnic make-up of your class?

Has anti-Semitism cropped up in any form when teaching about the Holocaust? If so, what form did it take and how did you respond?

Has Holocaust denial cropped up in any form? If it has, how did you respond?

Do you do anything to explore and undermine students' misconceptions and stereotypes of Jews and Judaism prior to teaching about the Holocaust?

In addition, 13 teachers were asked if they deal with rescuers and with Jewish resistance and five were asked whether they talk about victims of the Nazis other than Jews. Every teacher was guaranteed both personal and institutional anonymity.

THE FINDINGS

Basic Information

All teachers covered the Holocaust in Year 9 (with students aged between 13 and 15). While most spent between two and four hours on the subject, many spent considerably longer (in excess of five hours) and one or two considerably less. One teacher in a Catholic school allocated just 50 minutes despite stating that 'an awful lot of our children are extremely anti-Semitic and this has to be countered by teachers looking at the Holocaust.' Roughly half the sample did not wish to devote any more time to the topic. Those who did would like to have given more attention to the nature and history of anti-Semitism, the Nazis' non-Jewish victims and Jewish resistance. [A tendency to restrict coverage of the Holocaust to between two and three hours was also indicated in a more recent British study by Brown and Davies (1998). However, they point out that considerable time may be wasted as a result of history staff failing to liaise with colleagues in religious education who deal with much the same content.]

As far as resources are concerned, teachers mainly relied on textbooks and videos. Some, though, complained about the dearth of suitable print material for the less able. The video watched most often (at least in part) was the Genocide episode in the *World at War* television series, but the abridged version of *Schindler's List*, distributed free to schools by the Holocaust Educational Trust, also proved popular. The majority of teachers had either shown it in full to their Year 9 pupils, shown extracts, or made use of the accompanying documentary. Without exception, it had been well-received, but a couple of teachers refused to use it with their Year 9 pupils because they considered it 'too upsetting.' In relation to other resources, just four schools had sought out visiting speakers (in the form of Holocaust survivors) and even fewer had arranged visits of any kind, such as to the travelling Anne Frank exhibition. [N.B. At the time the research was undertaken there were no Holocaust museums or centres in the United Kingdom.]

Teachers' Attitudes

No teacher dissented from the view that the Holocaust ought to be included in the history curriculum and all but two were content to teach it at Year 9. One of the objectors said:

> In Year 9 they're not quite of the age to understand the real implications of what was involved in the causation and the effect. They can understand it on a very superficial level and we teach it at a superficial level at that time.

This teacher also feared the possibility of trauma if his Year 9 pupils were exposed to footage of the death camps. It was thus no surprise when, in reply to the question: 'How long do you spend teaching the Holocaust?' he remarked: 'I don't teach it at all. I just tell them to read the section in the textbook.'

Teachers saw the main advantage of Holocaust education in terms of alerting students to the dangers of racism. None of them, though, seemed to value its role in understanding the specific nature of anti-Semitism (cf. Dawidowicz, 1992). Indeed, one respondent said: '[In Year 9] we learn about the death camps, but we do it through the viewpoint of racism and not anti-Semitism.'

The possibility of causing distress was seen as the major disadvantage of studying the Holocaust. As one teacher put it: 'In principle there are no disadvantages (but) in practice it can be quite harrowing. It's very hard to strike the right balance between not shocking and alienating the children through fear, while making them fully aware of what went on.' A few teachers commented on the added problem of having Jewish children in the class. As one of them put it: 'You're particularly sensitive to Jewish students. Some have found it very difficult to cope with the lesson.' A couple of respondents had had to deal with concerned Jewish parents. In both cases the parents had objected in principle to the school teaching the Holocaust to their children as it was something they felt should be done at home.

Although no other disadvantages were identified, approximately one third of the sample felt uncomfortable when teaching the Holocaust. Some openly resented the time constraint. Others were concerned with the pupils' responses - either not knowing how to deal with racist remarks or fearing that students would not take the lessons seriously. A minority of teachers also worried that they would not succeed in conveying the true extent of the horror; an understandable anxiety in view of Stalin's quip about a single death being a tragedy and a million deaths a statistic. These sources of discomfort were all evident in Supple's survey (reported in Chapter 2). One source that she said nothing about, however, was that arising from teachers' ambivalent attitude towards Jews. In this connection, the head of one history department spoke as follows.

> I live in an area with a large Jewish population which presents me with a lot of personal problems and raises many questions about one's own response to Jewish people ... Given my reaction to them, where would I have stood if I had been in Nazi Germany? Would I have protested, or would I have been in an SS battalion? ... (There are also) questions about what has happened since the war, in terms of what Israel has done in defence of itself which, to some extent, mirrors what was done to them during the Holocaust (and) which has lost the Jews a lot of sympathy.

Issues Relating to Content and Pedagogy

One would have thought that familiarising students with the history of anti-Semitism was an essential prerequisite of understanding the Holocaust for, as a few teachers pointed out, 'You always get the question - why did people not like the Jews?' But despite such foreknowledge, over half the sample either made no reference to the subject or covered it inadequately. One teacher, when asked how much time he spent on the history of anti-Semitism, said: 'Almost none at all; it doesn't figure on the course,' while another confessed to spending 'about five minutes on it.' Although many stated that they would stress the fact that anti-Semitism was not just a twentieth century phenomenon, they nonetheless tended to restrict discussion of its form and development to events in Nazi Germany. They often insisted that this was not a matter of choice but the result of insufficient time. Other teachers, however, managed to devote the whole of the first lesson (often more than an hour) to the history of anti-Semitism and to the part played by the Christian church in preparing the religious backdrop to the Holocaust. With regard to the latter, staff in denominational schools were evenly divided between those who gave the issue serious treatment and those who dealt with it in an impressionistic way. Only one teacher though (in a Catholic school) confronted head-on the Church's role during the Holocaust. She was insistent on 'children (knowing) that one of the reasons the killing went on so long was the failure of moral spokespersons, such as the Catholic Church, to speak out against it.' Others were more defensive. For example, a teacher in an Anglican school said, 'I talk about the role of the Church in the persecution of the Jews but stress that true Christianity would not condone this.'

There was far more of a consensus on whether teachers should relate the Holocaust to recent political developments. The overwhelming majority did so and while some referred only to ethnic cleansing in the former Yugoslavia, rather more discussed the resurgence of racism across Europe. The value of the latter approach was illustrated in the following comment:

> When you start talking about Hitler and the Nazis, the low ability children say 'Oh, is it like the National Front?' I say 'Yes' and we talk about that and the rise of the neo-Nazis in ... Europe and the fact that foreigners often get blamed for a country's problems. At this point the children sometimes express their own racist views about immigrants coming over and taking our jobs and I try to question that.

None of those who spoke about Yugoslavia stressed the differences as well as the similarities between ethnic cleansing and the Holocaust and they may thus have succeeded in misleading their pupils about the nature of both tragedies. In contrast, the few teachers who referred to earlier genocides made clear how they differed from the Jewish experience under the Nazis.

There was also widespread agreement on the question of whether teachers should alter their approach to the Holocaust depending on the ethnic make-up of their class. The vast majority said they would make no concessions, but three felt differently. One stated that the high number of Asian students in his school led him to talk about the Holocaust in terms of racism rather than anti-Semitism. A second remarked that if he worked in an all-white area he would not draw comparisons between Nazi Germany and today's United Kingdom 'because the children wouldn't have any empathy with the social tensions,' while a third was affected by the substantial presence of Muslim pupils in his school. He believed that they 'had a very negative perception of Judaism and Jewish people,' but he did not spell out the implications of this observation for his own teaching.

Almost all respondents, when asked if they examine Jewish resistance, claimed that they did, although just how seriously they took the issue is another matter. Thus, one stated that 'it does not play a central part,' while another said: 'We touch on the Warsaw Ghetto.' Only one teacher mentioned the difficulties of armed resistance. Among the reasons given for excluding work in this area was a shortage of time and a lack of knowledge, factors that may also account for some teachers failing to broach the issue of rescue. Of those who did, the highly atypical Oskar Schindler was referred to most often and, in many cases, was the only rescuer referred to. Comparatively few teachers were asked if they drew attention to the Nazis' non-Jewish victims. All responded affirmatively, but some admitted to doing so in a fairly cursory manner.

The need for teachers to explore the way their pupils perceive Jews before tackling the Holocaust was underlined in the previous chapter. In the event, just two of them undertook this preliminary work, although it was unclear whether they set out to deconstruct religious as well as secular myths. Many teachers reported doing nothing to identify possible misconceptions among their pupils, either because they believed their pupils did not subscribe to any, or because they assumed that any such misconceptions would be tackled elsewhere in the curriculum (either in religious education or in personal and social education).

In response to the question on anti-Semitism, only one teacher mentioned an incident that was related directly to work on the Holocaust:

> One boy said, 'Not half enough of them (were killed).' I removed him from the class immediately, discussed what he'd said with the class, spoke to him at length about it, wrote a letter to his parents and he was put into detention. I suspect that he didn't really understand what he was saying because, when I spoke to him, he was a bit shocked.

Most respondents claimed that anti-Semitism had not cropped up in any form. None the less, a few recalled some pupils intimating in discussion that Jews were rich (implying, perhaps, that they thereby forfeited a degree of sympathy). A couple of teachers found this situation difficult to handle and went about it by pointing out that there are rich and poor in all communities. A third took the opportunity to inform his students, not altogether accurately, that the Jews in pre-war Poland were the industrial underclass.

Holocaust denial was sometimes raised by students and at other times by staff. Two students were remembered for having brought revisionist material into the classroom, while another, believed by the teacher to have joined the National Front, actually disputed the historicity of the Holocaust. However, after watching the video the teacher had shown as part of the lesson, 'he didn't pursue his argument.' There was a mixed response to the question, addressed to a sub-group of teachers, as to whether they should raise the issue of denial if their students failed to do so. One teacher's decision was prompted by the low expectations evident in some of his responses to previous questions. He said: 'I'm not sure whether at (Year 9) they could understand that issue. I think that for some, it might be quite a dangerous thing to do.' Those who felt differently were sometimes induced to act by the resources they worked with and sometimes by extraneous events. Thus, one teacher brought up the subject because it was referred to in the textbook he was using, while another claimed that his pupils were introduced to Holocaust denial material during their visit to the Anne Frank exhibition. However, a handful of staff broached the subject without any outside prompting and a frequent reason for doing so, as illustrated in the comments below, was to justify their teaching of the Holocaust.

> I've mentioned it to a group saying it's important we learn about the Holocaust because certain groups say it didn't exist.

> One reason I give them for teaching the Holocaust is that some people might say this never happened.

Significantly, only one respondent admitted to encouraging her students to think about the political identity of the deniers and the motives they have for their rejectionist stance.

Turning finally to the question of trauma, we are mindful that one of the canons of sound pedagogy is that the emotional impact of an educational resource must not inhibit the learning it is intended to facilitate. While the risk of this happening is manifestly high when teaching about the Holocaust, none of those interviewed had encountered pupils who had been traumatised as a result of studying the topic; many, though, had observed pupils who had clearly been moved. This was not a matter of concern for any of them. On the contrary, quite a few felt that students should be shocked and upset. In fact, the problem for some staff lay in evoking such a response. Desensitisation, resulting from frequent exposure to simulated violence, was singled out for blame. In the words of one teacher:

> When you see ... some of the more horrific (videos), it will touch some kids. The rest have seen worse in the horror movies - *Nightmare on Elm Street* and that sort of thing. They don't realise that this is actually happening to real people. Lots of them see it as just another video.

A Comment on Textbooks

The seven textbooks subjected to a content analysis can be seen as deficient in a number of respects. For example, while several allude to the history of European anti-Semitism, only one locates its roots in Christian theology. Most ignore the response of the international community to the fate of Europe's Jews and, in all of them, the plight of the Nazis' non-Jewish victims is dismissed in a sentence or two. Most mention armed Jewish resistance, but few make clear the difficulties involved and only one refers to the role of rescuers. A couple of books could also be faulted for reinforcing anti-Semitic stereotypes, or at least for presenting misinformation. The most widely used, for instance, states that: 'Prejudice against the Jews grew during the economic depression ... Many Germans were poor and unemployed and wanted someone to blame. They turned on the Jews, many of whom were rich ...' Now this assertion, while not contrary to fact, hardly gives an accurate account of the state of German Jewry at the time, for it makes no mention of the *Ostjuden* - the Jews from eastern Europe who, according to Landau (1992:92), 'frequently fell victim to unemployment and economic distress.' Another book asserts that 'Hitler's attempt to exterminate a race of people was only discovered once the Allies entered Germany and Poland.' This is an unfortunate statement, not only because it is historically incorrect, but because by concealing the fact that the British and American governments knew what was going on from the middle of 1942, students are effectively denied an opportunity to assess the culpability of the Allies for the extent of the devastation wrought by the Holocaust. Other instances of misleading text include the tendency for some books to talk about Jews *and* Germans, implying that Jews were an alien presence in the country rather than fully fledged citizens (as was the case prior to 1935) who were subsequently denied all human rights by their compatriots. There is also the matter of *Kristallnacht*, referred to in all seven books in the context of the shooting of the German diplomat, Ernst vom Rath, in Paris. However, only one of them explains why the diplomat was shot - essential information if students are not to be left with the impression that the pogrom was a justified response to an unprovoked attack.

A further misgiving relates to the way in which two of the books deal with Holocaust denial. As an exercise, one of them states: 'Some people today claim that the death camps are a propaganda myth. Do these sources provide reliable evidence that this is wrong? The other book presents students with essentially the same task. In neither case is there any comment on who these 'people' are, or on the nature of their agenda. Finally, in relation to content, it should be noted that none of the books recognise, even in passing, the positive aspects of Jewish history. The focus is exclusively on persecution.

THE ATTITUDES AND PRACTICES OF TEACHERS IN CANADA

The Canadian research, undertaken in 1998, was a replication of the English study. The sample comprised 23 history teachers (of whom 15 were Head of Department). There were 13 men and 10 women and all taught the Holocaust, as part of the compulsory Canadian history course, to students aged between 13 and 16 (in Grade 9 or 10). The teachers were drawn from 17 randomly selected high schools in and around metropolitan Toronto; five were Catholic and 12 non-denominational. The sample included two independent schools - one, non-denominational and all-girls; the other, Catholic and co-educational. The teachers were presented with the same questions as their English counterparts and were given the same guarantees of confidentiality.

THE FINDINGS

Basic Information

Just over two-thirds of the schools taught the Holocaust at Grade 10 (to 14- and 15-year-olds) with the remainder doing so at Grade 9 (to 13- and 14-year-olds). For the majority of teachers, the age range of 13 to 15 was deemed appropriate in that students were considered sufficiently mature, intellectually and emotionally, to handle the central issues. There was just one dissenting voice. A female member of staff in a suburban school that taught the Holocaust at Grade 9 would have preferred to wait a couple of years. She argued that:

> What you invariably face with young adolescents, and especially boys, (is) a fascination with the mechanics of extermination and it's difficult to get beyond that. It's not a TV show. This actually happened. This is people's lives that you're talking about. To get to that with some kids is not easy.

The mean length of time allotted to the subject was just over five hours, substantially longer than in England. However, the average masks a wide variation. While one teacher claimed to spend up to twelve hours and several others eight or nine, a handful took no more than a couple of hours to complete their coverage. In so doing, they mirrored the majority of textbooks used by the staff which were found to give the subject minimal attention, with one text exhausting its treatment in less than a page. Nearly half the teachers, including some who spent longest on the topic, wished for still more time. The issues they wanted to deal with in greater depth included the causes of the Holocaust (and particularly the history of anti-Semitism) 'the woeful response of the western powers' and the links between the Holocaust and more recent genocides. Jewish resistance and the role of rescuers were also mentioned in this context.

All the schools possessed and made use of videos or film footage but, as in England, there was disagreement over the suitability of some of this material. The emotionally powerful *Night and Fog*, for example, was believed by one teacher to be quite inappropriate for students in both Grade 9 and Grade 10. Instead, he preferred videos:

> that focus on the war in general, rather than specifically on the Holocaust, mainly because with the younger students much of that material is very graphic and I've always been wary of showing it. One of my colleagues has just shown *Night and Fog* to Grade 9. ... Every time I see it I cringe, so I'm nervous about showing it to 15-year-olds. I don't want to scare them to death.

The other side of the coin was put by a teacher (one of six) who did show the film at Grade 9/10 level.[†]

> I show *Night and Fog.* It's quite gruesome and some of the kids are in tears by the end of it. But what's too horrific? You've got to remind them that there are people out there saying this didn't happen and this is the video evidence.

In contrast to England in the mid-1990s, teachers in Toronto have long had access to a local Holocaust Centre (see Chapter 8). Many respondents made arrangements for their students to visit this facility and hear survivors speak; an experience that was universally valued. A couple of female teachers made additional use of survivor testimony in the form of Elie Wiesel's (1960) *Night.* One of them recalled that: 'The students were given (the book) to take home and read. ... Some of the girls this year have been in tears, but boys also respond to it very well.' Generally, however, the use of Holocaust literature by history staff was very limited; the only other title mentioned, and then only by a couple of teachers, was *The Diary of Anne Frank.*

Attitudes Towards Teaching the Holocaust

Nearly all the teachers were favourably disposed towards Holocaust education and there was little disagreement as to its merits. Almost a third of them talked about

---

[†] *Night and Fog* would seem an odd choice for teachers wishing to show their pupils film footage of the Holocaust, for it deals mainly with German action against members of the French resistance and as Novick (*op.cit.*, 103) points out, 'the word 'Jew' does not appear.'

learning from history and a further three referred explicitly to the opportunity to learn about racism and human rights. Their view was summed up by one respondent who said:

> (The Holocaust) allows us to move from history into issues of prejudice, discrimination and ultimately mass extermination. There's a superb opportunity to deal with values education.

An additional justification of Holocaust education, articulated by a few teachers, was simply that historical truth demands it. As one of them put it: 'to reflect accurately twentieth century history and ignore the Holocaust is a contradiction.'

When invited to consider the disadvantages of teaching the subject, just under a third were adamant that there were none, other than the frustrations of working within a limited time frame. Those who felt differently and whose views are represented below, included half-a-dozen (all female) who spoke of the evident pain caused to students who are unable to cope emotionally.

> It can be very disturbing. Some of our 13- to 15-year-olds get very upset, particularly when we visit the Holocaust Centre.

> Some young adolescents are clearly not prepared emotionally to deal with the horror of the Holocaust. The visual imagery overwhelms them.

> The disadvantage in the junior classes is that it's so depressing. The students get so emotionally drawn and drained. Also some of the younger students can't take it and they laugh, so we're very careful with the junior grades about the kinds of visuals we show. That's the only disadvantage.

For a few teachers the major drawback to teaching about the Holocaust in Toronto is associated with the city's position as the most ethnically diverse in Canada. According to the 1991 census, visible minorities comprise nearly a quarter of Toronto's population (Kelly, 1996) and some students from these groups were said to resent the privileged treatment accorded to the Holocaust when the suffering of their own ethnic community was ignored. [However, Reed and Novogrodsky's (2000) research, cited in Chapter 3, suggests that had we interviewed the students we might have heard a contrasting view.]

Finally, there was a handful of teachers who commented on the danger of 'Holocaust fatigue.' In the words of one Head of Department:

> I suppose it can be over-done. You get kids who, when you say 'we're going to do ...' say 'Oh, not again', because they've got it in English (and) they may have done it before. They may feel they are being manipulated, that somehow or other this particular event is being taught to death in the case of some kids.

The overwhelming majority of interviewees, when questioned about feelings of discomfort, said that they had none. However, a couple of women thought that their enthusiasm might create difficulties. One of them, possibly conscious of the dangers of preaching (Brehm, 1966) declared: 'I have no problem with the Holocaust other than that I feel very strongly about it and have to hold myself back.'

Issues Relating to Content and Pedagogy

Many respondents drew their pupils' attention to events in Yugoslavia and Rwanda, but there was a reluctance on the part of two or three to do likewise. In common with some of their counterparts in England, low expectations seemed to lie at the root of the problem. One teacher thought that students lacked the geographical knowledge required to understand the comparison, while another asserted that 'they're not cognisant of anything that's gone on, so I'd actually have to teach that before I could draw any connection.' A third teacher who eschewed comparisons said: 'I have a certain discomfort with comparative Holocaust studies. I think that in the Holocaust of World War II you're dealing with something historically unique.' Generally, however, teachers did make comparisons with earlier genocides, referring most often to the Armenian massacres, the fate of the Kulaks under Stalin and the treatment of First Peoples in Canada. The majority were at pains to stress the differences as well as the similarities between these various atrocities and the Holocaust, but the responses of a couple of teachers give cause for concern. One appeared to think that the main difference between the Holocaust and the situation faced by the Armenians and the Kulaks was that 'the Holocaust was a bigger atrocity.' The other believed that 'the powers that be in Serbia took a leaf out of Hitler's diary and pretty much did the same thing.' Although none of the textbooks made links with other genocides, they invariably referred to Canada's shameful role in the Holocaust noting, in particular, the government's refusal in 1939 to allow refugees from the *St. Louis* to disembark. The texts did not, however, focus on racism in present-day Canada. This tendency to overlook 'the home front' comes on top of the finding that only a minority of teachers raised the issue with their students.

In contrast, the entire sample responded affirmatively to the question: 'Do you talk about victims of the Nazis other than Jews?'. While two teachers confessed to doing so 'only briefly,' most appeared to take the issue seriously. There were many references to 'Gypsies,' homosexuals and Slavs, but interestingly, only one teacher mentioned Germans with disabilities and none spoke about Jehovah's Witnesses. Equally troubling is the comment from a teacher who seemed not to realise that in Nazi-occupied Europe it was only the Jews who were earmarked for total destruction. He said: 'We stress that Hitler's Holocaust included attacks on Gypsies and homosexuals so that the students see that there was a policy that was broader and capable of taking in enemies that they saw as needing to be wiped out.'

Asked whether they took cognisance of the ethnic make-up of their classes when teaching the Holocaust, the majority concurred with the respondent who said:

> It's important to know my students, but I wouldn't alter my approach (so much) as try to relate my teaching to the students' background. I have some black students and they are always deeply interested because they feel they are an oppressed minority and they are very aware of racism. If I'm aware of students' own ethnic backgrounds, I'm going to be able to relate what I'm doing much more directly to their own experiences and if I can tie their experiences, or even their second or third hand knowledge to what we're doing, it will make a better lesson.

One clear-cut example of tailoring a lesson to the ethnic composition of a class was given by a teacher who works in a school where the student body is almost entirely Jewish. He recalled that:

> After talking about the history of anti-Semitism, we discuss issues of racism and discrimination generally and I ask the students to bring in copies of the *Canadian Jewish News* to look at how the paper treats the Arabs. I wouldn't do that in a class that was just 50% Jewish, although I would do the same *kind* of thing.

A further example was provided by a teacher who had had experience of working with East European students.

> My previous school had a very high East European population (both first and second generation). These kids were carrying a cultural history that came from their own homes as well as from their ethnic language schools and you have to be sensitive to where they're at - what they are coming to you with in their minds. I'm not suggesting that you compromise your historical goals in terms of teaching what happened, but you have to be sensitive to the conflict you may be causing in their minds and even in their homes. I know for a fact that some of these kids had grown up in homes that were rife with anti-Semitism and it was incumbent on me to be aware of that.

When asked how the presence of such students would affect her teaching, she replied: 'I would probably go back more into history and deal with the history of anti-Semitism and you have to spend more time on the Christian church and more time on Russian history in terms of the Russian empire.'

As in England, many teachers did not treat the history of anti-Semitism seriously in Grade 9, or Grade 10, although they generally made it clear that 'Hitler did not arise in a vacuum.' Nearly half the sample just 'touch(ed) on the role of the Church' and most of the others did nothing. The reasons were varied. In one case it was due to time constraints; in another it was attributed to the religious ethos of the school, the teacher maintaining that: 'It's difficult ... in a Catholic school to make the association.' For a further two respondents, the failure to tackle anti-Semitism was due to ignorance - not of church teachings - but of Jewish history. Significantly, there was no mention of the long-standing link between the Church and anti-Semitism in any of the five textbooks that were used in the schools.

While some students' misconceptions may have been undermined as a by-product of learning about the Holocaust, none of the teachers approached the subject by first exploring their students' beliefs about Jews and Judaism with a view to deconstructing them if necessary. As was the case with the generality of teachers in England, the justification for failing to do so was that the students did not subscribe to any ill-informed beliefs.

> I've never run into those misconceptions ... In my experience, the students here don't have any particularly strong feelings about Jews or any other ethnic group.

> We really don't have to [explore their views on Judaism] because the Catholic church and its teaching right now see the Jews as the chosen people and their religion is deeply connected to ours.

Although most teachers referred to both resistance and rescue, a small number eschewed any mention of these topics 'because of the time frame' and a few admitted to treating them in a rather shallow way for the same reason. In fact, the majority of those who commented on Jewish resistance did no more than 'touch on' the Warsaw ghetto; they were silent on uprisings in the death camps and in other ghettos. Some, however, did broach the issue of spiritual resistance. On the subject of rescue, Oskar Schindler was named most frequently and far more often than other well-known cases such as Miep Gies, the Danish fishermen and Raoul Wallenberg. Incidentally, none of the teachers made their pupils aware of the difficulties of resistance and the penalties attaching to rescue. This may reflect the fact that resistance is alluded to (fleetingly) in only one textbook while rescue is not alluded to in any of them.

None of the respondents believed that any student they had taught had been traumatised as a result of studying the Holocaust. Many recalled instances where students had been deeply affected by what they had seen but, as in England, this was not considered a problem. With regard to film footage, teachers generally warned students of what they were to encounter, allowing them to opt out if they wished.

Teachers reported half a dozen anti-Semitic incidents arising from their work on the Holocaust. In some cases the offender was sent to the principal, but a couple of teachers pointed out that expressions of hostility towards Jews were often objected to by other students. While it is not known whether the latter type of intervention was successful, the potent influence of the peer group in adolescent culture suggests that its use could prove more effective than a recourse to punishment. Anti-Semitism, in the form of Holocaust denial, had been experienced by just one teacher when working in a Catholic school with large numbers of Polish and Croatian students. Recollecting the experience, he said: 'I (was) called a liar and threatened with my life by people from these communities because (I told them) there was a Holocaust in their country.' Most teachers maintained that they would raise the issue of denial if their students did not and the reason most commonly advanced was that 'students are going to come across it. They know about Ernst Zündel.' However, one teacher had never mentioned the subject, believing that 'bringing it up might have a negative effect on those who are bordering on the maturity level' and two others said that they had discussed denial with their students in the past but did not do so as a matter of course. In contrast to the English sample, the majority claimed to make clear the political identity and the motives of the deniers, although a few appear to have failed to prepare their students adequately to recognise the danger. One of them, for example, makes a point of *not* informing his students that the deniers are neo-Nazis. Instead he tells them that 'Zündel is wrong. Here's the evidence ... You can't deny video footage, tattoos on arms, people breaking down.' But such a response ignores the fact that some deniers do indeed dismiss all such evidence, while others dispute its connection with a policy of extermination (Lipstadt, 1993).

Summary

A degree of unease emerges from the two studies described in this chapter. In the first instance it will be recalled that while almost all the teachers claimed to be committed to Holocaust education, they failed to treat it as a vehicle for understanding the nature of anti-Semitism. In fact, most did little or nothing on the history of this form of prejudice. They may thus have made it difficult for their students to see the Holocaust in perspective and to comprehend why the Jews, rather than some other minority group, were selected as the Nazis' principal victims. A further concern stems from the fact that so few teachers recognised the need to assess their students' perceptions of Jews and Judaism prior to starting lessons on the Holocaust. Instead, they *assumed* that there was no need for such preliminary work, maintaining that their students were either free from the sort of misconceptions that would inhibit their learning or would have any false beliefs challenged in other areas of the curriculum. The data presented in Chapter 4 argues against the first of these assumptions, while a lack of evidence makes us wary of the second.

Some of our concerns stem from the comments of relatively few teachers. A small number, for example, appeared ignorant of critical differences not only between the Holocaust and other genocides but between the suffering of different groups under the Nazis. Several teachers also held unreasonably low expectations of their students' intellectual capacity and emotional resilience. As a result, they were reluctant to show informative film footage and hesitant about raising the issue of Holocaust denial. An additional anxiety arises from the minority of teachers who seemed content to devote a minimal amount of time to the Holocaust. The issue here is not just the attitude towards racism of all kinds that is implicitly conveyed, but the impoverished understanding of the subject that is bound to ensue. Insufficient time inevitably meant superficial coverage of a range of topics such as resistance and rescue and, as we have seen, the problem of inadequate treatment was compounded by the errors and omissions in textbooks.

Chapter 6

Holocaust Education and Citizenship

The contribution that a knowledge of the Holocaust can make to citizenship education is self-evident, for one of the latter's principal purposes in a multi-ethnic society must be to expose racism as an anti-democratic force (Osler, 1999). Coming to terms with the Holocaust allows students to appreciate racism's destructive potential and its inherent capacity to target *any* ethnic group, if sufficiently powerless. It permits an awareness that the roots of racism are often historically embedded and that both socio-economic and psychological factors can play a catalytic role in igniting underlying tensions. It can also deepen an understanding of the processes of stereotyping and scapegoating, show that racism has a universal appeal and encourage reflection on what needs to be done to diminish its influence. And not the least of the benefits of studying the Holocaust is the opportunity it affords to ponder the consequences of individuals and organisations failing to make the right choices when confronted by evil. Whether these advantages are real, however, in the sense of affecting the way students think has yet to be determined, for it is not known what, if anything, students learn about citizenship in general, and racism in particular, when they engage with the Holocaust as history. Equally important is that we do not know what aspects of their learning they retain over the longer term. It was in order to find out that the following small-scale investigation was undertaken.

The sample was an opportunistic one comprising 43 mixed-ability Year 10 students aged between 14 and 16. All were volunteers and were drawn from six urban secondary schools in south-east England. Twenty-two of the students were female and 21 male, with just over half belonging to 'visible' minorities. All of them had studied the Holocaust about a year before participating in the research and had opted to take the history examination in their General Certificate of Secondary Education.

Semi-structured interviews were conducted on an individual basis. The questions were categorised as follows.

Knowledge of the Holocaust

> Tell me what you know about the Holocaust?
> Were Jews the only group singled out by the Nazis for persecution?
> Why did it happen?
> Could it have been prevented?

Why was the rest of the world reluctant to take Jewish refugees in large numbers
   from Germany?
In respect of the Holocaust, are there any heroes?

Racism and the Holocaust: Making Connections

What is a racial stereotype? What was the Nazi stereotype of the Jew?
What is a scapegoat? Who were the scapegoats in Nazi Germany? What were they
   blamed for?
What does the Holocaust teach us about racism?
Could there be a Holocaust (not necessarily of Jews) in England? [If 'yes', what
   would have to happen to bring it about? If 'no,' why not?]

Preventing a Repetition

Should racist political parties be allowed to stand in general elections?
Should people of your age learn about the Holocaust?
Should young people everywhere learn about it, or just those in countries directly
   affected?

Personal Impact of Learning about the Holocaust

Has studying the Holocaust changed you in any way? [If so, how?]
What has the Holocaust taught you about being a good citizen?
What does the Holocaust teach us generally - about life and about people?

[Due to lapses of concentration on the part of the interviewer, some students
were not asked certain questions.]

THE FINDINGS

Knowledge of the Holocaust

Partly to put the students at ease, they were initially invited to say whatever they
knew about the Holocaust. Despite the unfocused nature of the question, many of
the comments (either made spontaneously, or in response to a subsidiary question)
related to the number of victims. While the majority gave a figure in the region of
six million, others were very wide of the mark, ranging in their estimates from 'a

thousand' and 'six to ten thousand' at one extreme, through to 'thirty million,' 'forty million' and even 'hundreds of millions' at the other. One student was not sure whether it was 'six million or six thousand'; another did not know whether it was two or twenty million and a third was not prepared to venture a guess. The very low estimates are particularly troubling, for if one of our priorities in teaching the Holocaust is to demonstrate where racism can lead, we must ensure that our approach to the number of victims is unequivocal. Anything less risks reinforcing the credibility of far-right agitators like Jean-Marie Le Pen (leader of the *Front Nationale* in France) who attempt to trivialise the Holocaust by referring to it as 'a footnote in history.'

One of the more obvious ways in which the Holocaust sheds light on the nature of racism is by making clear that those it infects do not necessarily direct their venom at visible minorities alone. To gain a sense of the extent to which knowledge of the Holocaust had helped promote this understanding, the students were asked if Jews were the only group persecuted by the Nazis. Table 6.1 details their response.

Table 6.1 Groups other than Jews persecuted by the Nazis

Group	Number of references
Black People	11
People of non-Aryan appearance	9
Roma and Sinti (referred to as 'Gypsies')	7
Disabled	7
Communists	7
Non-Germans	5
Homosexuals	3
Adherents of religions other than Judaism	3
Arabs/Muslims	2
Slavs	2
Russians	2
Mentally ill	2
Other	2

In view of the thinking behind the question, it is disturbing to note so few references to the Slavs, the Roma and Sinti and those who suffered for reasons unrelated to ethnicity. Moreover, four students thought that Jews *were* the Nazis' only victims and one was unable to answer. Although a matter of concern, this finding is not altogether surprising, for as we have seen, the majority of textbooks currently available in English secondary schools tend to deal with the Nazis' non-Jewish victims very briefly. Equally disturbing is the large number of references to 'Black people.' Although historically accurate - the Nazis sterilised hundreds of 'mixed-race' adolescents - it is improbable that the students had this particular breach of human rights in mind when addressing the question. More likely is that many students in the United Kingdom, whatever the context, automatically associate racism with colour. (See also Modood, 1989.)

Table 6.2 shows their responses to the question, 'Why did the Holocaust happen?'

Table 6.2 Why did the Holocaust happen?

Reason	Number of references
Hitler wanted an Aryan race/ believed Jews were an inferior race	12
Envy (of Jewish success)	10
Jews responsible for Germany losing the war	9
Hitler was intolerant of difference	5
Hitler disliked Judaism	3
Jews responsible for economic problems	2
Jews were of different appearance/ dark skinned	2
Other	11
Not sure/Don't know	9

Arguably, one of the more important things that needs to be learnt about anti-Semitism in the modern world is that it is historically embedded. It is not, as implied by a number of responses to the question, a natural by-product of envy; nor is it an inevitable accompaniment to crisis in the domestic economy or to defeat on the battlefield. And it is not something either that can be summoned up at will to justify the genocidal fantasies of a deranged tyrant. The students reacted to the question with a serious lack of historical consciousness in failing to realise the significance of the rich vein of anti-Semitism that has coursed through European culture for centuries. None of them mentioned the role of the Church in fomenting a psychological climate that would help to nourish an anti-Semitic campaign. Such an omission is consistent with the survey of teachers' attitudes and practices in England referred to in the last chapter. For what emerged from that survey was that more than half the teachers either made no reference to the legacy of anti-Semitism when discussing the historical background to the Holocaust, or covered it quite inadequately.

We recognise that there is no simple or straightforward answer to the question of why the Holocaust happened. Even so, we are concerned that so few students alluded to the catalytic role of either the economic depression or the twin psychological blows of Germany losing the war and having to endure the humiliation of Versailles. The basis of our concern is that an essential element of citizenship education must be an appreciation of the threat posed to ethnic minorities by industrial collapse and the puncturing of national pride. The following 'explanations' of the Holocaust reveal how, in many cases, this understanding was entirely lacking.

> The Nazis didn't like the Jews because of their religion, their appearance - they weren't Aryan - and because they didn't have a homeland.

> Hitler wanted Germany to be the best and he wanted to get rid of anybody who would get in his way. That included people with disabilities, but mainly the Jews.

> Hitler wanted to start the master race - blond-haired, blue-eyed, intelligent people. He felt that Jews, Gypsies and the mentally ill were inferior. He just wanted to eliminate them from the human race.

Two of these comments reflect what may have been a widespread view among the students; namely, that Hitler and the Nazis were, in a critical sense, acting alone. None of them showed an awareness that Nazi ideology appealed to a diverse range of interest groups within Germany, all of whom supported Hitler in his quest for power. In areas such as commerce and the professions, there were obvious benefits to be derived from eliminating Jewish competition; an important point to get across to adolescents in a number of western countries at the present time in view of the success achieved in precisely these spheres by sections of the ethnic minority population.

The question of whether the Holocaust could have been prevented was intended to test the students' knowledge of possible sources of opposition to government policy and to probe their understanding of the power of ordinary citizens to influence national developments through participation in the democratic process. The question was addressed to every student and it can be seen (in Table

Table 6.3 Could the Holocaust have been prevented?

Verdict	Number of references
Yes if:	
Other countries had acted	15
The Germans had not voted Hitler into power	8
The country had not been in such a bad economic or psychological state	4
People in Germany and outside had known what was going on	3
The Jews had fought back	1
The Catholic Church had intervened	1
No because:	
Hitler had a lot of power	4
Hitler was mad/determined	1
Jews powerless to fight back	1
No reason given	2
Other	5

6.3) that over a third of them referred to the failure of other nations to intervene. [One spoke about refugee policy between 1933 and 1941; the rest had in mind military action by the Allies.] The precise nature of this action was not spelt out, but from the standpoint of education for citizenship, cognisance of foreign involvement of some kind indicates that students' attention had been drawn to the consequences, in terms of human rights abuses, that may flow from national governments adopting a parochial attitude to what goes on in the world at large. This recognition is clearly welcome, for the notion of responsible citizenship has to embrace global as well as local concerns. Less welcome, however, was the paucity of references to opposition from non-military sources. There was only one comment, for example, critical of the role of the Church. The data also make clear that relatively few students seemed to acknowledge the possibility of opposition through the ballot box, for only eight of them stated that the Holocaust could have been prevented had the German people not voted for the Nazi party. Although others may have considered this a point too obvious to make, there has to be a suspicion that some students are unaware of the dangers immanent in democratic government. On a related matter, it should be noted that none of the students argued that the Holocaust might have remained a figment of Hitler's imagination had anti-democratic political parties been proscribed.

Other important issues were highlighted by some of the responses to this question. In the first place, it is essential, when learning about the Holocaust, that young people do not end up blaming the victims for their plight. On the contrary, if antiracist goals are to be realised, students must identify with the victims. They may be less inclined to do so, however, if they see them in an unheroic light, as the one student who blamed the Jews for not fighting back is likely to have done. A further concern, was the failure of many respondents to appreciate the contribution that economic prosperity and national pride can make to social cohesion. On a more positive note, there was clear evidence that at least some students of this age can see the danger in granting unlimited authority to the executive branch of government. Four of them claimed that the Holocaust could not have been prevented 'because Hitler had too much power.'

We turn now to assess the students' understanding of the universal nature of racism. We do so in the context of events following the Nazi take-over in 1933 when Jews began leaving Germany in search of a more secure future. They tried to leave in ever-growing numbers as the decade wore on, but found it increasingly difficult as one country after another tightened its immigration procedures. The students were asked to speculate on the reasons why so many countries were reluctant to accept an influx of German Jews. In posing the question, we were particularly interested in whether they would offer an explanation in terms of anti-Semitism, thereby demonstrating their awareness of its ubiquity throughout the western world. The data show that just over a quarter of them thought that the international community's largely unsympathetic response could have been motivated by hostility towards Jews. Among their comments were the following:

> If people weren't racist they would freely (have) accepted Jews coming to their country. In every country there's a minority of racism in everybody.

> They might have felt that their jobs and economies would have been taken over by the Jews if they came in large numbers.

> They were also afraid that if the Jews came into their country, the same thing would happen - the Jews would get the power and the wealth.

Two responses to the question were couched in terms of what would now be referred to as the 'new racism' (Barker, 1981), with its emphasis on ethnic minorities as a source of cultural conflict rather than a cause of socio-economic disintegration and racial defilement.

> If you take in a very large number of refugees of a certain kind, it can have quite a significant effect on the culture of that country.

I think everyone has some sort of hostility towards people who aren't the same and they didn't want to be overrun.

In Chapter 4 we stressed that if students are to be helped to act against racism, rescuers need to be seen as role models. It was this assumption that prompted us to ask: 'When you think about the Holocaust, are there any heroes?' Almost half of those questioned did not identify any heroes in the Holocaust and among those who did, the majority failed to conceptualise heroism in ways that had anything to do with a willingness to suffer in the interests of justice. Students who regarded Jews as heroic were impressed merely by the fact that some had survived. Quite a few hailed the efforts of rescuers, often mentioning Oskar Schindler by name, but there were only three who thought of heroism in terms of a preparedness to pay the ultimate price for acting in accordance with the dictates of conscience. The following transcript is illustrative.

Interviewer: In respect of the Holocaust, are there any heroes?

Student: Yes, all the people who protected the Jews.

Interviewer: What makes them heroic?

Student: If they'd been found out, they would have been killed. They're risking their lives for what they think is right.

Racism and the Holocaust: Making Connections

We now examine what the students learnt about two of the fundamental components of racism, namely, stereotyping and scapegoating. We begin with the former, for as we have suggested, one of the advantages of Holocaust education is the ease with which it can deepen a knowledge of stereotyping by showing that it does not always take the same form or have the same origins. The students were asked, 'What is a stereotype?' and, following an explanation if necessary, 'What was the Nazi stereotype of the Jew?'. It has to be a matter of some concern that less than half the sample claimed to be *au fait* with the concept. Moreover, when the students were later questioned about the image of the Jew in Nazi ideology, around 20 per cent said they did not know or had forgotten. The most frequent response was that Jews were 'evil.' However, when asked to elaborate, the students invariably displayed a lack of real understanding asserting, for example, that '(Jews) were bad because they weren't Aryan' or because 'they were horrible to people.'

If it is important to demonstrate to students that stereotypes can assume forms other than those with which they may be familiar, we should not ignore some of the comments evoked by the question, 'What was the Nazi stereotype of the Jew?'. The fact that a couple of respondents said that Jews were 'stingy' and another referred to them as money-lenders, should alert teachers to the power of existing knowledge to interfere with and inhibit new learning. The same applies to another respondent who may have had Afro-Caribbeans and South Asians in mind when she said 'The Jews were taking the (Germans') jobs and homes.'

To explore their knowledge of scapegoating, the students were presented with three questions; namely, 'What is a scapegoat?' 'Who were the scapegoats in Nazi Germany?' and 'What were they blamed for?'. Again, only around half the sample were familiar with the concept. The rest either admitted that they did not know or proffered an 'example' which confirmed that they did not know. Six students could not identify the scapegoats in Nazi Germany and one-third of those who could, did not know what the Jews were alleged to have done to warrant the contumely heaped upon them.

The question, 'What does the Holocaust teach us about racism?' revealed that while a few students said it teaches us 'that racism is wrong,' many more were concerned with where it can lead. Thus:

> It teaches us that we shouldn't be racist because it just gets larger and larger, from one person to a group and it starts getting more violent and you start killing people.

> How it can get out of control and end up in mass killing. It's not just calling names and having a fight.

> It has to be stopped before it escalates into something worse. If Hitler had not been allowed to go so far in the beginning, the Holocaust wouldn't have happened.

Other members of the group had learned different, but nonetheless important lessons.

> It teaches us that if a lot of people see racism as a way out and a way to enhance their own lifestyle, then a lot of people will go for it. Also, you can get a lot of supporters by telling people what they want to hear.

> People who hold racist views shouldn't be allowed freedom of speech.

It also transpired from replies to this question that around half a dozen students had learnt (or, at any rate, had not been disabused of) the fundamental misconception that, under the Nazis, Jews suffered because of their religious beliefs.

Links between the Holocaust and contemporary racism were probed when the students were asked whether there could be a Holocaust (of any ethnic minority) in England. Opinion was more or less evenly divided between those who admitted the possibility and those who rejected it. The former were challenged to say what would have to happen for such a catastrophe to arise and consistent with an earlier finding, there were just five students who referred either to economic collapse or to national trauma as potential catalysts. As the comments below demonstrate, those who thought a Holocaust could not occur in England did so for reasons that some might regard as a dangerous cocktail of naivety and complacency.

> After the Holocaust people's views have changed so much it won't happen.

> A lot of people have lessons about what could happen so that would probably prevent it.

> The Holocaust is taught and people actually know about it. In this day and age, people can see the warning signs.

The possibility of a Holocaust in England was also discounted on the grounds that racism is not sufficiently entrenched in the country to act as a viable launching pad.

> There doesn't seem to be racism on a large scale.

> I think people are more open-minded now and there aren't as many racist people around. People get on a lot better now, no matter what colour they are.

> There's not enough craziness in the country to do it. If someone came to power and said 'go and do this', most people would just say 'no'.

Preventing a Repetition

The students were asked whether overtly racist political parties such as the National Front and the British National Party should be allowed to contest elections. Three-quarters of them were opposed to the idea and in 13 cases, some of which are recorded below, the opposition was justified in terms of what had happened in Nazi Germany.

> If they got elected it would cause a lot of trouble for victims of their racist views, like Hitler and the Jews.

> If that party gets power, it would be like Hitler coming into power again. Maybe another Holocaust might happen.

> It could be like Hitler again, not with the Jews this time, but with minorities from Arab, African and Asian countries.

Among others who opposed the participation in elections of racist political parties, most did so either because of the perceived unfairness of discriminatory politics or because of the inanity of elevating racial considerations above all others.

We looked next at whether the students felt sufficiently strongly about Holocaust education to campaign on its behalf should its future ever be put in jeopardy. Asked if people their own age ought to learn about it, almost all were in favour, with more than half underlining its role in preventing a recurrence.

> Definitely, to prevent it happening in the future. If people know the causes and the reasons why it happened - what should have been done and what could have been done, then, in the future, if anything like this happens, we will be able to step in.

> It's important that we learn about the Holocaust because we don't want to get into a situation like that again. Before the Holocaust people were worrying about what was happening in Germany, but they didn't do anything to stop it. Because of the Holocaust we've learnt that maybe, if you want to deal with things like this, you ought to deal with them before they get blown up into big things.

The rest of the students made no reference to the future. They saw the value of engaging with the Holocaust solely in terms of becoming more aware of the past. But however they construed its benefits, those who supported the idea of their peers having to learn about the Holocaust were subsequently asked if it should be taught throughout the world or only in those countries that had been directly affected. Nearly all of them favoured the universal option. Some did so because they recognised the potential for racism within every society; others because they wished to teach people everywhere about their global responsibilities.

> Everyone should know, to prevent it happening in other countries as well.

> It becomes a world situation when it happens because the world has to step in.

Personal Impact of Learning about the Holocaust

The first of the three questions in this category required the students to consider how, if at all, learning about the Holocaust had changed them. Just over a third claimed not to have been changed in any way, some adding that the experience had merely broadened their general knowledge. Of those who believed they had been changed, seven stated that it had made them think more deeply about the nature of racism. For example:

> I didn't realise that racism could go that far and that one man could have that much power and ruin so many lives.

> Before I did the Holocaust I didn't know how bad racism was.

It's made me think about racism a lot more.

Cited below are some of the remarks made by a further nine students who intimated that learning about the Holocaust had influenced their behaviour, or was likely to do so.

It's probably changed me in the way that I treat people who aren't the same as me, like people who are a different religion. It's not fair to start picking on them if they haven't done anything to me because that's like what happened then. It's what Hitler did - just picking on easy prey.

It's made me realise that you don't class people as a race; you take them as they come.

It's helped me to think more about life. How precious life is. We shouldn't be so quick to stereotype people; we should maybe take a second to think.

It's strengthened my views on what I believe is right and wrong. I didn't know about the Holocaust before I studied it. I was shocked when I found out this had happened in the twentieth century. Also, it's taught me to stand up for what I believe in.

Two students who claimed to have been affected by their work on the Holocaust expressed views that are especially noteworthy. The first is from a boy whose background is both Arab and Muslim. [For a similar reaction from university students, see Levi, 1998.]

When I was small, watching the news and seeing what the Jews do in Israel, I hated them. After I studied the Holocaust, I remembered what happened to them, how they got into Palestine, so it changed me a lot to think of them as normal people and they didn't deserve what they got. They're human and they have the right to live in the country.

While it should be no part of Holocaust education to foster sympathy for Zionism, it is essential, as has been pointed out, to cultivate among the young an interest in citizenship and human rights that extends beyond their own country's geographical borders. However, there is no virtue in an ill-informed interest and to the extent that knowledge of the Holocaust is able to dispel some of the myths surrounding the Arab-Israeli dispute, its educational value is enhanced. The second comment that warrants a mention came from an Asian girl who said of her encounter with the Holocaust: 'It's made me more against the Germans.' Although she was the only student in the sample to articulate an anti-German sentiment, her experience clearly warns of a potential danger in studying the subject; namely, its ability to foment and intensify prejudice and not just diminish it.

The penultimate question required the students to reflect on what they had learnt about good citizenship as a result of engaging with the Holocaust. For the most part, the responses were variations on the twin themes of not judging a book by its cover and ensuring that everyone is treated with equality, respect and fairness. A minority of students, however, chose to focus on the importance of taking personal responsibility for their actions. For them, the Holocaust teaches that:

> You have to make up your own mind. You don't just follow someone who may bring you something you want but who's going to do something that you don't agree with.

> (You should) not just listen to what one person says, but listen to what everyone says and then think it all over and think about the most logical way to overcome the situation.

> (I should not) accept what everyone else thinks is right - to have my own opinion and also to speak out for those who are being affected.

> (You shouldn't) listen to others. Judge people by what they are, not what other people think of them. The German people thought about Jews the same as Hitler, so they were bad to the Jews.
> *Interviewer:* What should the German people have done then?
> They should have judged the Jewish people by themselves.

To give the students a final opportunity to consider the relevance of the Holocaust for citizenship education, they were asked: 'What does the Holocaust teach us generally - about life and about people?' Not surprisingly, the responses were diverse and, to a considerable extent, reiterated points made earlier. Some, though, were made for the first time and they are reproduced below. The opening comment, for example, was the only occasion on which reference was made to the role of bystanders.

> It shows how cruel humans can be to one another and that people just turn a blind eye to it.

> It tells us that people should have equal rights, but how at some times in history, people didn't have those rights and how not having those rights affected their lives.

> That there are evil geniuses like Hitler. If the Holocaust had never happened, we would have thought that something that terrible could never happen. It teaches us that it can.

> There are some people who will use their power to do evil and they can't be stopped in a lot of cases unless action is taken very early.

Concerns and Implications

This chapter set out to explore what a group of 14- and 15-year-olds learnt about citizenship as a result of studying the Holocaust as history. Specifically, the data analysis was undertaken in order to gauge both their knowledge of the Holocaust and the impact of that knowledge on their understanding of racism. We propose to highlight and comment briefly on some of the more salient findings and on their pedagogic implications.

One of our principal concerns derives from a suspicion that many students interpreted the Holocaust as the work of a lone individual. This way of thinking is, perhaps, an extreme example of the 'rotten apple' theory of racism (Henriques, 1984) in which the phenomenon is treated as nothing more than an aberration based on personal inadequacy. To help counter such a view, teachers must make their pupils aware of the different interest groups that stood to gain from a Nazi take-over in Germany and show how these various groups contributed to Hitler's success.

No less important is the need to stress the nature and significance of the deeply ingrained tradition of anti-Semitism in the country and this will necessarily entail making reference to its roots in Christian theology. The urgency of this need is indicated by the fact that not a single respondent remarked on the critical role of an anti-Semitic culture when discussing the origins of the Holocaust and only one respondent referred to the non-intervention of the Church when asked if the Holocaust could have been prevented. Emphasising the centrality of anti-Semitism has the added advantage of enabling students to place the economic depression, the military defeat and its humiliating aftermath in context, treating them as catalysts rather than as underlying causes of the Holocaust. It is also worth noting that many students did not seem to realise (probably because they had not been taught) that anti-Semitism *in other countries* was a major obstacle to Jewish emigration and must bear a responsibility for contributing to the Jewish death toll. As we suggested in the previous chapter, it is imperative that this fact be made known if the Germans are not to be branded as singularly lacking in humanitarianism and uniquely evil in respect of racism.

The small number of students who demonstrated an understanding of the plight of the Roma and Sinti and the Slavs has also been identified as a concern. Teaching about their fate is not just a matter of recognising a historical truth (Cornwell, 1996), or of illustrating the vulnerability of relatively powerless peoples, for the suffering endured by these groups provides teachers with an opportunity to help their pupils understand more about the nature and consequences of stereotyping. Such work would seem to be an urgent priority bearing in mind that less than half the sample had any real understanding of this critical concept. The same can be said for scapegoating, for it will be recalled that similar levels of ignorance were observed in relation to this concept too.

Another concern that we have commented upon involves the failure of the majority of students to recognise the role of rescuers as heroic. It would be quite wrong, as we have intimated, to teach the Holocaust in such a way as to give the impression that the number of rescuers was anything other than a tiny fraction of those who preferred to turn a blind eye. Honouring their bravery and defiance, however, is another matter, not least because promoting good citizenship demands, among other things, that we encourage the young to adopt morally defensible positions and to act in accordance with them, regardless of the consequences.

Judging by their responses to the questions and especially by their support for Holocaust education, there can be no doubt that many of the students benefited considerably from learning about the attempted annihilation of European Jewry. The experience expanded their knowledge of racism and made them think more deeply about their responsibilities as citizens. Other students, however, appear to have acquired, or at least, had not been disabused of some fundamental misconceptions about the Holocaust and, as a result, had learnt less than might have been wished about the nature and impact of racism.

Chapter 7

Holocaust Curricula

Ten years ago, in a widely reported study, Lucy Dawidowicz (1992) expressed serious misgivings over the quality of Holocaust curricula in the United States. She was particularly perturbed by what she saw as their inappropriate aims, amounting in some cases to 'outright political indoctrination' and by their potentially harmful pedagogy and misleading content. In respect of the latter, she complained of some giving the impression that anti-Semitism was an invention of the 1930s, while others ignored its links to the teachings of Christianity. Dawidowicz also reproached curricula that 'routinely charged (the United States) with indifference to the fate of the Jews during the war (failing to mention) the belief of US Government and military officials that the only way to stop the murder of the Jews was to defeat Hitler on the battlefield' (*ibid.*, 70). In order to gain insight into the contemporary relevance of her critique, we examine, in this chapter, two curricula that are currently in widespread use; namely, the second edition of *Facing History and Ourselves*, which enjoys a high profile throughout North America and the first edition of *Lessons of the Holocaust*, a teaching pack that has been sold to more than a thousand secondary schools in the United Kingdom. These curricula have not, however, been selected solely on account of their popularity, for we also aim in this chapter to illustrate the different priorities of Holocaust educators. As the analysis unfolds, it will become apparent that while some curricula are principally concerned with the Holocaust as history, others operate with a broader remit, seeking to promote political literacy and moral development as well as historical knowledge (Shoemaker, 2003).

LESSONS OF THE HOLOCAUST

We begin with *Lessons of the Holocaust*, a set of resources produced jointly in England in 1997 by the Holocaust Educational Trust and the Spiro Institute. The contents comprise two handbooks, an hour-long video and a number of flashcards, display posters and reproductions of a range of primary source documents. One of the handbooks, *Information for Teachers*, is divided into three sections. The first covers the historical background to the Holocaust and was written by the distinguished academic Robert Wistrich. Part one, entitled 'Jews, anti-Semitism and the rise of Hitler,' begins with a survey of Jewish communities in Europe on the eve of the Second World War, pointing out that the majority were to be found in the east, especially in Poland and the Soviet Union. It is stated clearly that two-thirds of Europe's pre-war Jewish population was destroyed by the Nazis. The sub-section dealing with 'The Jewish people: religion and culture' opens with a brief excursion into ancient times, adumbrating the links between Judaism and Christianity and usefully reminding readers that 'Jesus, Mary and the Apostles were all Jews.' However, the 'golden ages' of Jewish cultural achievement (such as occurred in Spain between the tenth and twelfth centuries) are largely overlooked, for the focus switches rather abruptly from the biblical period to the late nineteenth century, where Jewish patterns of settlement in eastern Europe are described and the mass migration to the West explained in terms of pogroms and poverty. Reference is made to the situation of the Jews in Germany at the outbreak of the First World War and it is stressed that the half-million strong community felt deeply connected to German society. Their sense of belonging is conveyed by commentary on the Jewish contribution to German culture, science and commerce, while sacrifices on the battlefield, for the Kaiser and the fatherland, are detailed as testimony to the patriotism of German Jews.

In contrast to Dawidowicz's findings, much space is devoted to the history of anti-Semitism, the handbook making clear that the roots of this prejudice can be traced back to Greco-Roman times. The nature and manifestations of medieval anti-Semitism are covered in some depth, as are the writings and the lethal influence (on German Protestants) of Martin Luther. Attention then focuses on the late nineteenth century accusation that Jews are intent on overthrowing the established order - a myth significantly invigorated by the Bolshevik takeover in Russia. The narrative discusses the anti-Semitic ideology that Hitler imbibed in Vienna, the origins of the Nazi party and the publication of *Mein Kampf*. Reference to the electoral successes of the party completes the opening section.

Part two confronts 'Nazi Germany's anti-Jewish policy: from exclusion to expulsion, 1933-1939.' The various sub-sections deal first with the steady increase in anti-Jewish discrimination aimed at removing Jews from German cultural and economic life. The Nuremberg Laws of 1935 are then addressed and their purpose explicated. Much attention is given to the events of 1938 and especially to the shooting of Ernst vom Rath in Paris and the Nazi party's response in the form of the *Kristallnacht* pogrom. Other issues raised include Jewish emigration from Germany and the reluctance of many of the participant nations at the Evian conference to relax their immigration quotas. Among countries singled out for criticism are the United States and 'those with large territories and sparse populations within the British empire.' It is in the context of Jewish emigration from Germany that the ultimately fruitless journey of the SS *St. Louis* is recounted. Part two concludes with a comment on the controversy over whether or not Hitler intended to destroy the Jews from the outset and with a statement on the failure of German public opinion to protest at the Nazi regime's anti-Jewish measures.

Part three, 'The road to genocide 1939-1942,' starts by recalling Hitler's prophecy of January 30, 1939, that in the event of war, 'the Jewish race in Europe' would be annihilated. It goes on to describe the invasion of Poland, the setting up of ghettos and the formation of Jewish Councils, some of whose leaders, it claims, were corrupt. The text alludes to the fate of a few prominent Council leaders such as Jacob Gens, Mordecai Rumkowski and Adam Czerniakow, but there is no discussion of the indictment levelled by Hilberg and Arendt accusing the Councils of complicity in the Holocaust. A brief description of life and death in the ghettos is provided with particular mention made of the lengths the Jews went to in order to preserve their cultural traditions. The conflict between Jewish youth and the Jewish Councils over how best to respond to the Nazis is commented on as a prelude to a discussion of Jewish armed resistance, the latter concentrating mainly on the Warsaw ghetto uprising. Nazi alternatives to extermination, such as the Madagascar plan, are outlined before attention turns to the invasion of the Soviet Union. At this point, readers are apprised of the activities of the *Einsatzgruppen* (liquidating Communists, partisans and Gypsies as well as Jews) and to the enthusiastic collaboration in the killing of Lithuanians and Ukrainians. The reasons for locating the death camps in Poland are explained and the range of non-Jewish victims is made clear. There then follows an extended discussion of Nazi policy towards the Slavs with consideration given to how it differed from policy towards the Jews. The fate of the Roma and Sinti is also treated seriously. Again, differences with the Jewish situation are identified and specifically, it is claimed that in contrast to the Jews, 'not all Gypsies were earmarked for destruction.' [Unfortunately, the value of this important distinction is undermined by one of the "Questions for Discussion' that appears towards the end of the handbook. It asks, 'Who were the other victims of Hitler's extermination plans?']

Part four considers 'The Final Solution, 1942-1945.' It begins with the Wannsee conference, stressing that all those in attendance were 'educated and "cultured" individuals.' Denmark, Italy and, with some qualification, Bulgaria, are praised for their resistance to the Final Solution and tribute is also paid to the government of Finland for its refusal to comply with Germany's demand to hand over its small Jewish population. There follows a short account of the fate of the Jews in other European countries and the eager participation of the Austrians in realising that fate - rendering the continent *judenrein* - is deemed particularly noteworthy. The Hungarian situation receives extended coverage and the case of the United Kingdom is raised in the context of its immigration policy and its involvement in Palestine. The role of the United States during the Nazi era does not escape critical scrutiny and it is suggested that high levels of anti-Semitism in the country played a major part both in its mean-spirited response to Jewish immigration and in its reluctance to mount any sort of rescue operation. However,

Dawidowicz's criticism, that Holocaust curricula in the United States, fail to mention their government's defence of its policy on rescue does not apply to *Lessons of the Holocaust*, for the text states explicitly the Allies' belief that 'only a speedy and complete military defeat of Hitler' could save the Jews. The concluding sections of Part four underline the Nazi obsession with annihilating the Jews of Europe (overriding in importance the country's military needs) and the complicity of the German people. It is argued that the vast majority of ordinary Germans made no protest although they must have known what was happening.

With the historical overview complete, the handbook devotes a couple of pages to consider the 'Lessons of the Holocaust'. This rubric is somewhat misleading as much of the section merely summarises what has gone before. When, in the final paragraphs, reference is made to the lessons to be learnt, the list is predictable and bland. Among other things, we are told that the Holocaust is not just a German problem for there have been other genocides since 1945; that 'hatred of others ... can lead only to group violence and atrocity'; that 'each individual is responsible to his or her conscience' and that 'there should be no place for racism and anti-Semitism in a truly tolerant, civilised society.' Following these so-called lessons is a postscript covering the aftermath of the Holocaust. Two issues are raised. One deals with the parlous state of East European Jewry as reflected in the murder of over 500 Holocaust survivors in Poland during the first twelve months that Europe was officially at peace. The other, war crimes prosecutions, is discussed with reference to the Nuremberg trials, that began shortly after the war and continued in the late 1940s, and the trial of Adolf Eichmann in Israel in the early 1960s.

The second part of the handbook offers comprehensive guidance on teaching the Holocaust in the context of the National Curriculum for England and Wales. Much of what is written is now out of date, but the lesson plans, in both their shorter and longer versions, remain very useful. Bearing in mind the limited time that most teachers feel able to devote to the Holocaust, the shorter version containing four lessons, would seem to be especially valuable. The lessons focus on (a) The roots of anti-Semitism (b) Making Germany free of Jews (c) The road to genocide 1939-1942 and the Final Solution 1942-1945 and (d) Jewish resistance, rescue and post World War Two developments. All the lessons last an hour and include extracts from the accompanying video (see below). They are broken down into sub-stages with each one allocated a stipulated amount of time. Every lesson has clear learning objectives and is differentiated by ability. In addition to the recommended lessons, guidance is given on how other curricular areas - English, geography and religious education - could be taught so as to broaden students' knowledge and understanding of the Holocaust. Some of the suggestions for religious education, however, are worrying, because they focus heavily on the rituals and teachings of Judaism and thus risk conveying the impression that Jews were targeted by the Nazis for religious reasons. The handbook ends with questions for discussion, a page of suggested essay titles and a bibliography consisting of teaching texts, academic histories of the Holocaust and survivors' biographies . The latter are identified as suitable either for adults or for a younger audience.

The video *Understanding the Holocaust* is comprised of ten segments, most lasting five minutes, and the narrative closely follows the historical notes for teachers. Thus, the first three segments deal with *The roots of anti-Semitism*, emphasising the Jewish origins of Christianity and making reference to the writings of Luther. The shadow cast by anti-Semitism in the nineteenth century features prominently and reference is made to Hitler's early life, and the history of Germany between 1918 and 1933. The next three segments, *Making Germany free of Jews*, focus on the anti-Jewish discrimination, the setting up of Dachau with its motto 'tolerance is weakness,' the imprisonment of the regime's political opponents and the burning of books, particularly by university students. Other topics covered include the Nuremberg Laws, the attempted emigration by Jews and Hitler's fury at Jesse Owens' success in the 1936 Olympics. Mention is made of official dissemination of anti-Semitism in schools (partly through primers such as *The Poisonous Mushroom*), and the influential role of *Der Stürmer* is underlined. The final segment of *Making Germany Free of Jews* deals with the invasion of Austria and the subsequent humiliation of that country's Jewish population, the *Kristallnacht* pogrom and Hitler's infamous speech at the end of January 1939.

The last of the three main sections of the video, *Towards Extermination*, examines life in the Warsaw ghetto and draws attention to the forced-labour, the starvation rations and the devastation wrought by disease. Spiritual resistance is commented on and there is footage of the 1943 ghetto uprising. The video then tracks the stages of the Final Solution following the German invasion of the Soviet Union. There are shots of the *Einsatzgruppen* in action, the gas vans and the death camps. The involvement of the *Wehrmacht* and of non-Germans in the killing is not ignored and viewers are informed of Himmler's speech about the need to keep the Final Solution secret. The importance of the Wannsee conference is made clear and, in connection with the Auschwitz camp, the video records for the first time the non-Jewish victims of the Nazis. There are references to the 'selection,' the medical experiments of Mengele, and to Elie Wiesel's first night in the camp recalling the death of his mother and sister and his subsequent loss of religious faith. The concluding segment of the video lasts about fifteen minutes and deals with the Jews of Hungary; it also considers the broader issue of the Allies' response to the Holocaust and specifically, whether they could have done more, after 1942, to stop it. There is footage of the liberation of the death camps by the Russians and of the concentration camps in Germany and Austria by western forces. Against a background of horrific imagery of walking skeletons and decayed corpses, students are reminded, in a sombre peroration, that the Holocaust occurred in a modern, developed country but would never have happened without the two thousand year legacy of anti-Semitism and the willing collaborators in other countries.

Various teaching aids are intended to be used in conjunction with the historical sections of *Information for Teachers*. They include maps, documents, eyewitness accounts, literature, press articles, rescuers' case studies and resistance testimonies. All are contained in the second handbook, *Lesson Resources.*

Maps

Among other things, the ten maps show the areas where Jewish resistance fighters were particularly prominent, the ghettos and camps in which the Jews revolted between 1942 and 1945 and the extent of the persecution of the Roma and Sinti. A couple of the maps, however, are of questionable relevance to the Holocaust. One outlines the history of the Jews of the United Kingdom between 1660 and 1914; the other (seemingly more germane) is headed 'Non-Jewish victims of Nazi rule.' It is intended to complement the section of *Information for Teachers* dealing with the way the Nazis treated their ideological opponents, but is actually concerned with the sites of German reprisals for partisan activity.

Documents

The 25 documents that have been selected contain quotations from anti-Semitic tracts over the last two millennia and from speeches and reports by high-ranking Nazi officials. There are also facsimiles of Nazi party edicts and legislation and *Einsatzgruppen* accounts of the extermination of the Jews. Between them, the documents help to illustrate the Christian origins of anti-Semitism; the rise of racial anti-Semitism; the Nuremberg Laws, *Kristallnacht* and the fate of the Jews in Lithuania and the Ukraine. The nineteen articles of the United Nations Convention on Genocide are also included.

Eyewitness Accounts

There are six of these accounts. One is from Albert Friedlander who, as an 11-year-old boy in Berlin, witnessed the events of *Kristallnacht*. Another is taken from the diary of an SS doctor, Johannes Kremer, who worked at Auschwitz in 1942. Details of Kremer's life accompany the extract from his diary and similar potted biographies preface the testimony of Rudolf Hoess, the first commandant of Auschwitz, and the brief excerpt from Anne Frank's diary. There is a lengthy and moving account from Gena Turgel, a Jewish woman born in Poland in 1923, the youngest of nine children. She recounts her experiences of Auschwitz and of Bergen-Belsen. There is also a passage from a speech made by Winston Churchill in a House of Commons debate in 1935. It is, however, an odd inclusion for, unlike the others, Churchill had not seen at first hand the situation he was describing.

Rescuers' Case Studies

There are nine cases of individuals who, either on their own or as members of a group, saved Jews. Although Oskar Schindler is cited along with Raoul Wallenberg, and other well-documented examples, ordinary men and women from across Europe, whose exploits are not at all well known, are also featured. They are treated in a way that enables readers to comprehend the range of factors that motivated the rescuers of Jews.

Resistance Testimonies and Chronology

This section is arguably the least useful, for 'resistance' is defined so broadly as to all but lose its meaning. The first item, for example, is a letter sent from a leading German Rabbi, Leo Baeck, to the Reich Minister of War in 1935 asking that Jews be allowed to serve in the Wehrmacht. It is difficult to see why it is deemed to constitute an act of resistance. It is certainly not one likely to impress adolescents and prompt them to empathise with the victims. The same can be said about the reference to Rabbi Daniel who requested permission from a German officer to speak to his congregation just before they were to be shot. He wanted to tell them to accept their fate with equanimity. It would not surprise us if some students saw such a response as an act of craven compliance rather than as anything resembling resistance. There then follows an extract from an article written in 1941 by the Protestant theologian Martin Neimöller. The piece is certainly a case of defiance as it is critical of the Nazi regime, but we do not see what it has to do with *Jewish* resistance, the subject of this section of the handbook. In fact, out of the nine items that are included, only two relate to what most readers would instantly recognise as acts of Jewish resistance. The first is Mordecai Anielewicz' account of the Warsaw ghetto uprising; the second is the testimony of Jack Kagan who escaped from the Polish town of Novogrudok (now in Byelorussia) and joined a Jewish partisan group. [A chronology of armed Jewish resistance in ghettos and camps between the beginning of 1942 and the end of 1944 is included as an addendum.] However, as was pointed out in Chapter 4, resistance is not restricted to the armed or the spiritual and this is recognised in the extract from Chaim Caplan's Warsaw diary, the suicide note from Shmuel Zygielboym and in a poem penned in the Thereseinstadt ghetto.

Literature

Three poems have been selected. One is from a young boy in the United States and relays his thoughts on learning about the Holocaust half a century after it occurred. A second is taken from Primo Levi's *If This is a Man* and the third was written in 1943 by a non-Jewish Pole active in the underground. It would have been helpful had some guidance been given to teachers as to when and how these poems might be used to best effect.

Press Articles

The last substantive section of the handbook contains 26 newspaper articles, the majority of which have been culled from the British press. The cuttings run from 1933 to 1945 and deal, among other things, with anti-Jewish discrimination, violence against Jews in Germany, the book burning of 1933 and the Nuremberg Laws barring the Jews from German citizenship. Among the collection is a valuable piece from the *Manchester Guardian* rebutting Nazi claims about Jews dominating the professions and poor Jews from the East swamping the country. There is also a very revealing article taken from a popular British newspaper in 1938 manifesting the anti-Semitism it professes to abhor.

A number of display posters, flashcards (mainly in the form of monochrome photographs) and reproduced documents complete a teaching pack that appears, for the most part, to be very different from those in the United States lambasted by Dawidowicz (1992). Certainly, there can be no suggestion of political indoctrination or historical inaccuracy, although the references to Christian anti-Semitism could be considered misleading in so far as no mention is made of post-war developments in the Church's attitude towards Judaism. Dawidowicz's strictures in relation to pedagogy are equally redundant, for *Lessons of the Holocaust* is silent on this matter. Indeed, the pack can fairly be accused of failing to recognise the importance of pedagogy; the authors appearing to see their role as providing no more than a straightforward historical account with appropriate resources and with suggestions as to how other subject areas might complement the history. Students are presented with a narrowly-focused academic curriculum giving them no opportunity to explore their own feelings towards the political, social and moral issues involved. Nor is there any scope for debating contentious matters such as the co-operation between the Jewish Councils and the Nazis. That said, the narrative is accessible and, in relation to the Nazi era, comprehensive, although it is regrettable that in its broad sweep of Jewish history, it glosses over the glorious episodes (cf. Kochan *op. cit.* Biale, 1986). Teachers will undoubtedly find the resource section valuable and they are likely also to welcome the lesson plans (especially in their abridged form) and the recommended cross-curricular links.

FACING HISTORY AND OURSELVES

Background

Facing History and Ourselves (FHAO) is a United States-based educational foundation that started as a local grassroots organisation in Brookline, Massachusetts in 1976. Since its inception it has become highly influential and now reaches over half a million students in North America annually. Although best known for its resource book *Holocaust and Human Behaviour*, the foundation also publishes and disseminates other teaching material, distributes videotaped interviews of survivor testimony, provides educational programmes and collaborates with universities on research projects. It receives funding from both private and public bodies.

Facing History and Ourselves: Holocaust and Human Behaviour (1994)

The resource book differs from many other Holocaust education curricula in that it is not a short-term programme or a prescribed set of lessons. Rather it is a lengthy (576 page) compilation of readings and suggested follow-up activities that offers what the authors hope will be a 'long term intervention.' It is designed for use in social studies, literature, art and science lessons although 'most teachers incorporate (it) into a history or language arts course' (Skvirsky, 2000). The purpose of the resource book and its attendant educational supports is stated in the Introduction. 'FHAO is devoted to teaching about the dangers of indifference and the values of civility by helping schools confront the complexities of history in ways that promote critical and creative thinking about the challenges we face and the opportunities we have for positive change' (p. xx). Central to its mission is the concept of civic literacy defined as 'the competence to participate in democratic communities, the ability to think critically and act with deliberation in a pluralistic world, and the empathy to identify sufficiently with others to live with them despite conflicts of interest and differences in character' (p. xvii). Clearly, *Facing History* has a far broader remit than *Lessons of the Holocaust*, for while the latter aims to provide no more than a historical overview, *Facing History* has, as one of its core concerns, the fostering of political and moral education.

However, to develop civic literacy *Facing History* asserts that it is important to examine carefully historical events and particularly important to examine the Holocaust - a time when democracy failed and civility was abandoned. The Holocaust is selected in preference to other events in the past because 'in no other history are the steps that resulted in totalitarianism and ultimately genocide so carefully documented not only by the victims but also by the perpetrators and bystanders' (p. xviii). Although the authors claim that the Holocaust was unique, they insist that as a case study it can illumine universal questions about the necessity for tolerance and the desirability of a civil society. In support of this view, they cite the words of Eva Fleischner, Catholic theologian and educator: 'We can attain universality only through particularity: there are no shortcuts. The more we come to know about the Holocaust ... the greater the possibility that we will become sensitised to inhumanity and suffering whenever they occur' (p. xvii). The authors acknowledge their debt to Jacob Bronowski and Hannah Arendt who both wrote about the relationship of thought to action. Arendt did so after attending the trial of Adolf Eichmann where one of the things that struck her most forcefully was the man's apparent thoughtlessness. As a result, she asked: 'Could the activity of thinking as such, the habit of examining ... be among the conditions that make men abstain from evil-doing or even condition them against it?' (p. xxi). In the end, Arendt concluded that thinking in itself does not lead to action and that informed judgment constitutes the bridge between them. *Facing History* thus offers 'students a variety of perspectives and (helps) them sift through differing, and at times conflicting, points of view before asking them to make wise judgments' (p. xxii). The curriculum sets out to enhance cognitive growth and specifically to complicate students' thinking. It does so by making use of the Socratic method and by encouraging the habit of viewing the world from different perspectives. Students are stimulated to think about the choices they have as individuals and about the consequences of the choices they make.

As far as classroom relations are concerned, *Facing History* suggests that an autocratic didactic style, in which the teacher enacts the role of an authority figure or expert is not the kind of pedagogy it supports. Instead, it maintains that 'learning is always a collaborative process and one that blurs the line separating student from teacher' (p. xxx). Discussion therefore plays a critical role in the curriculum and teachers are advised of the importance of creating a climate of trust and mutual respect.

Organisation and Structure of the Resource Book

The resource book has eleven chapters each structured in a similar fashion. They begin with an overview that outlines the key concepts and themes of the chapter. This is followed by a number of readings (usually between 15 and 20) that explore the content of the chapter in greater depth. Although teachers are recommended to choose those that match the perceived needs and interests of their students, as well as the learning objectives the students are pursuing, some readings are seen as developing important concepts and teachers are instructed not to omit them.

The readings sometimes summarise historical events; more often, they provide commentaries on primary sources citing the words of ordinary people or persons of renown. The latter include writers like Maya Angelou, Elie Wiesel and Aharon Appelfeld and scholars such as Lawrence Langer and Martin Gilbert. At the end of each reading are a number of open-ended questions and occasionally other activities and advice to teachers under the heading 'Connections.' They 'are designed to build curiosity, develop habits of enquiry, promote critical thinking, encourage research and foster an understanding of the relationship between various ideas and concepts' (p. xxix). It is suggested that teachers urge students to record in a journal their answers to the questions raised in these sections and to leave space in the journal for subsequent reflection. The aim is to document changes in the students' thinking over the duration of the course.

Content

The introductory chapter explores the relationship between individuals and the society in which they live. It also begins the exploration of many of the central questions developed in the programme concerning identity formation and the tensions set up between the maintenance of individuality and group membership. The associated readings provide students with a conceptual framework crucial to understanding the Holocaust. They focus on different aspects of racism such as the notion of 'race' itself, stereotyping, prejudice and conformity. Strangely, though, when discussing the issue of religious stereotyping, the authors assert, without any qualification, that 'religion is part of our identity' (p. 43).

Chapter 2, 'We and They,' outlines the ways in which various nations have defined their identity. The process of definition is considered significant because it determines membership of the nation's 'universe of obligation.' This term, coined by Helen Fein (1979), refers to the circle of individuals and groups 'towards whom obligations are owed, to whom rules apply, and whose injuries call for (amends) by the community.' The associated readings examine how the United States, France and Germany have, at different times, employed the concept of nation to define some groups as lying within the universe of obligation and others as lying beyond it. For example, reference is made to the American Declaration of Independence and the groups it considered to be part of the nation. (Native and African Americans were defined 'out.') There are several readings about Germany between the wars, showing how the legacies of scientific racism, eugenics and the myth of the Aryan race contributed to excluding Jews from the national universe of obligation. One of the readings deals with the complexities of Jewish identity and is valuable because it makes clear that for anti-Semites, Jews are a racial group. However, it also includes a quotation claiming that Jewishness is 'some mixture of ethnicity and religion.' Such a claim is to be regretted because, as we have stated on previous occasions, it reinforces the myth that all Jews murdered by the Nazis were, in some degree, committed to Judaism.

Chapter 3 marks the beginning of the case study and examines the choices people made in Germany after the First World War. Most of the readings focus on the devastating impact of the war on the German nation, on how the Treaty of Versailles was experienced by Germans and on the consequences of the economic slump. They also cover Hitler's rise to power, citing extracts from *Mein Kampf* to illustrate that anti-Semitism and the demonisation of Jews were present in Hitler's thinking and writing long before he became Chancellor. From the standpoint of combating anti-Semitic stereotypes, there is a particularly commendable narrative, based on Niewyk's (1981) work, debunking the Nazi claim that Jews controlled the German economy.

The next few chapters deal with how the Nazis transformed Germany 'into a totalitarian state by turning neighbour against neighbour in order to break the moral backbone of a citizenry and *why* the German people allowed them to do so' (p. xxvii, original emphasis). Chapter four details the steps from the Weimar Republic to the early years of the Nazi government. Among the readings are some relating to the day that Hitler became Chancellor - from individuals who were repelled by what they saw and from those who were attracted to both the pomp and the false promise of Hitler's 'new' beginning. Other readings look at the role of the churches (including the Jehovah's Witnesses), the take-over of the universities and at who, besides the Jews, were defined as lying outside the Nazi state. In this context, reference is made to the Roma and the gay community and to the party's ideological opponents. There is an account of the Nazi book burnings which notes that the first to go up in flames were studies on homosexuality from the Institute of Sexual Science. Students are asked to consider why books are considered dangerous and why the Nazis began their purge with those about gays.

Readings that help students to reflect on why the German people allowed their country to become a totalitarian state are introduced in Chapter 5. To aid their understanding, the text describes the much-quoted research by social psychologists Stanley Milgram (1974) and Philip Zimbardo (1972), examining how authority figures and institutional settings influence obedience. Students are presented with questions about its nature and about how it differs from conformity. In-depth coverage is also given to the use of propaganda in the fields of sport, art and education. Its effects on human behaviour and especially on the thinking of the young is underscored and one of the suggested follow-up activities usefully directs students to think about the difference between education and indoctrination.

Chapter 6, entitled 'Escalating Violence' focuses on how individuals and nations defined their universe of obligation in the late 1930s and on the consequences of those definitions. It asks why the German people did not stop Hitler when he threatened minorities at home and why world leaders failed to take a stand when he turned his aggressive intentions towards neighbouring countries. In the context of these questions, the readings chronicle Germany's withdrawal from the League of Nations, her march into the Rhineland and subsequent annexation of Austria. They also cover *Kristallnacht* and the steps that led to it - the expulsion of East European Jews and the violent response of Herschel Grynspan. To emphasise further the consequences of being outside a universe of obligation, the euthanasia programme and the targeting of Roma and Sinti are recalled along with the ghettoisation of Jews throughout Eastern Europe. Students are urged to think why there was no coherent response by the international community to these ominous developments and why democracies in particular are reluctant to intervene in the affairs of other nations when human rights are under threat. Against the backdrop of the Evian conference, students are further urged to reflect on the concept of a political refugee and on how the West currently treats those who seek asylum.

'The deliberate murder of one third of all the Jews in the world' is considered next and teachers are warned early on about the dangers of simulation games (cf. Dawidowicz). Students are introduced to a vocabulary that will assist them to conceptualise the premeditated and wholesale murder of a people and, at the same time, acquaint them with the ways in which the Nazis hid their intentions and actions behind a sanitised language. The euphemisms they employed such as 'liquidate' for murder and 'bath houses' for gas chambers are listed and examined. The text then looks at the murders committed by the *Einsatzgruppen* and at Christopher Browning's seminal study of Reserve Police Battalion 101. The emphasis that Browning places on conformity is a theme that is referred to several times in the resource book and gives rise to a number of student-based tasks such as contemplating the nature of cowardice. Other readings rely heavily on survivor testimony of 'life' in the ghettos and the camps (with quotes from Primo Levi, Elie Wiesel and Charlotte Delbo). Although non-physical resistance warrants barely a mention, armed uprisings in the ghettos of Kovno, Cracow and Warsaw and in the death camps of Treblinka and Sobibor are covered in some depth. At the same time, students are made aware of how the victims were deceived by propaganda and lies to the very end thus depriving most of any real chance of resistance.

After detailing the events of the Holocaust and clarifying the choices available to the victims and perpetrators, Chapter 8 considers 'the choices open to everyone else once the Holocaust began' (p. 363). The first few readings deal with what the average person in the affected countries knew, a question well illustrated by the case of those who lived near the Mauthausen concentration camp in Austria. We are told that the townspeople smelled the night burnings and saw hair and other human remains in the vicinity, but chose to believe the official explanation and to stay silent. The topic recommended for discussion is why the locals made this choice and, more generally, why people sometimes feign ignorance of the evil that surrounds them. The text then moves on to examine the role of rescuers and challenges students to focus on what they teach us about human behaviour. It also encourages them to review their working definition of a hero and ask themselves whether the Talmudic saying, 'Whoever saves one life saves the world entire' applies to Schindler and others who sought to protect the innocent. The final part of the chapter includes, among other things, a critical commentary on the role of the churches in the Holocaust and an analysis of Allied policy in relation to rescue and the bombing of Auschwitz.

Aftermath and Meaning

Chapter 9, 'Judgment', explores questions related to responsibility for the Holocaust and for the war itself. Students are asked to address issues such as 'Who should be judged? - the individuals who gave the orders; the people who carried out those orders (or) those who allowed it to happen?' (p. 424). They are also asked to contemplate the purpose of a trial; whether it is to punish the guilty, avenge the victims or act as a warning. The chapter leaves students in no doubt that many issues of justice vis à vis the Holocaust involve, or have implications for, other countries. One reading, for example, questions whether the Americans were right to grant leading Nazi scientists immunity from punishment if they emigrated to the United States. Another focuses attention on the morality of Israel's kidnapping of Eichmann, while a third is concerned with genocide as a crime against humanity. It requires students to indicate which of various atrocities can be described as genocide in terms of the United Nations 1948 convention and then sets them the task of deciding how the international community should react 'in the face of knowledge that a government is massacring its own people' (p. 460).

With an emphasis on prevention, Chapter 10 considers the power of our memories to shape the present. It draws attention to different ways, including relativisation, in which cultures attempt to suppress what they wish to forget. The readings address issues relating to the preservation of memory, explaining, for example, why many survivors feel a need to testify. They also deal with issues of memorialisation, the nature and politics of Holocaust denial and the problems that many young Germans have in coming to terms with their past. Some readings consider the need to face the legacy of other painful historical episodes such as the enslavement of African Americans and the genocide of the Armenians. In respect of the latter, the reasons for the failure to confront memory are discussed at some length.

The final section of the resource book, 'Choosing to participate' looks at what is needed for a democracy to succeed. The views of Abraham Lincoln and Vaclav Havel on this matter are recorded and the readings dwell on acts of good citizenship necessary for a 'civil society.' Individuals held up as role models include Marian Wright Edelman, the first African-American woman to practise law in Mississippi and founder of the nation's leading lobby group devoted to the needs of children. There is an account of a physician who chooses to practise medicine in the inner city and of a former Klansman, C.P. Ellis, who left the movement to work in politics alongside an African-American woman. This chapter, in common with Chapter 1, emphasises individual participation and responsibility and the penultimate reading focuses on the actions and worldview of perhaps the most famous Holocaust survivor, Elie Wiesel. It is suggested that students imagine who he would accept as his neighbours and what he would regard as the boundaries of his community. The last reading is the well-known poem by Robert Frost which encourages students to consider taking 'the road less travelled by', stressing the individual's responsibility for moral decision-making.

Critique

The resource book deals with so many aspects of the Holocaust, linking them to other atrocities in the past and to human rights abuses in our own time, that it is hard to imagine how a meaningful engagement with the material could fail to enhance students' political awareness and sharpen their moral sensibilities. It is thus no surprise that Brabeck *et al.* (1994) working in the United States, found the programme helpful in raising the level of moral reasoning of more than a hundred eighth grade students and did so without adversely affecting their psychological health. The results no doubt reflect well on the recommended methodology of journal keeping and especially the use of a 'double entry' journal which seems to be an ideal means of ensuring a prolonged encounter with the issues. However, *Facing History*, is not beyond criticism, as can be seen in Deborah Lipstadt's (1995) comments on the danger inherent in what she refers to as its 'fast-and-loose comparative approach.' She writes:

> My discomfort has less to do with the way the Holocaust is approached and more with the context into which it is placed. Facing History addresses a broad array of injustices including the Armenian genocide and American racism. ...
> The problem with this approach is that it elides the differences between the Holocaust and all manner of inhumanities and injustices. Though (the authors) are adamant that this is not their intention, it is hard to imagine how a teacher constructing a curriculum based on Facing History could adopt any other mode.
>
> (Lipstadt, 1995:27)

How teachers actually deal with this problem is an empirical matter and in the absence of relevant research data we are unable to comment further.

We can, however, comment on what appears to be a major omission in the curriculum. The authors rightly feel that it is important for students to see the Holocaust in historical perspective and to this end they refer to the annals of anti-Judaism. One of the early readings is devoted to this topic and although it discusses, among other things, the life and times of Jesus, it surprisingly makes no mention of the accusation of deicide that has been levelled against Jews over the centuries. In the associated Connections section, there is an allusion to the papal declaration *Nostra Aetate* issued in 1965, but nothing is said about the document absolving Jews from responsibility for the death of Jesus. In view of the success achieved by the recently released and highly controversial film *The Passion of the Christ*, this omission ought to be rectified as a matter of urgency.

Rather less serious is what seems to be a bias in the historical content, for while we were unable to find any reference in the text to the debate between the intentionalists and functionalists over the genesis of the Final Solution, we note that the authors actually come down in favour of the former. They write: 'In 1939, as Hitler planned the murder of the Jews ... ' (p. 497). We believe that in so far as the curriculum has, as one of its central aims, to teach the history of the Holocaust, students and teachers should be made aware of this major controversy and that *Facing History* has taken a stand in relation to it. However, we recognise that in recent years opinions have begun to converge and that the controversy itself has no implications for citizenship education.

A further limitation of the curriculum is that while it involves students in thinking critically about historical and political events, it does so only at the level of the individual. It fails to examine collective political action in the form, for example, of organised political dissent, labour movements and human rights groups. Moreover, nowhere in the curriculum is there a critique of the liberal democratic state as the ideal. Citizenship is promoted within the framework of such a state and volunteerism is the suggested way in which students are encouraged to participate.

Despite these criticisms, we find that the *Facing History* approach overall has much to commend it. Not least is the fact that it is transparently honest about its intentions, for the resource book states clearly that 'Facing History ... is committed to content that furthers democratic values and beliefs' (p. xxi). This candour, in our view, is fitting for a pedagogy that aims to be egalitarian. If students are expected to be open about their evolving values and opinions, instructors should be equally open about their approach and the values they espouse. The resource book itself constitutes a rich and useful reader that encourages students and teachers to become intellectually and morally engaged with the Holocaust and its aftermath. In addition, it fosters critical thinking and challenges participants to make connections between past errors and their own moral and political choices. To quote one high school teacher, it is a programme that 'honours duality; process and product, head and heart, history and ethics' (p. xxii).

Chapter 8

Holocaust Museums

As we pointed out in the Preface, the last two decades have witnessed a surge in the number of Holocaust museums around the world and especially in the United States. It might be thought axiomatic that such museums are a good thing; indeed, an invaluable asset and particularly so for teachers who lack expertise in the subject or who may be struggling with flawed or insufficient textbooks and other resources. The value of Holocaust museums, however, ought not to be taken for granted for, in common with all teaching aids, they have the potential to mislead as well as enlighten. They may, for instance, give the impression that Jewish history is synonymous with persecution or that all pre-war European Jewish communities were essentially the same, at least in terms of their shared commitment to religious belief and ritual. They may unwittingly reinforce stereotypes and myths about Jews or, at any rate, do nothing to challenge them. They may pay scant regard to rescuers or minimise the suffering of Hitler's non-Jewish victims and when dealing with the perpetrators, they may fail to distinguish Germans from Nazis or understate the extent of collaboration in occupied Europe. There is also the possibility that museums may present a sanitised account of their own country's record on anti-Semitism and particularly its response to the victims of Nazism. In the light of such potential pitfalls, we focus in this chapter on the contribution to Holocaust education made by two museums - Beth Shalom in England and the Holocaust Education and Memorial Centre of Toronto.

Beth Shalom Holocaust Memorial Centre

Beth Shalom ('House of Peace'), the United Kingdom's first Holocaust museum and remembrance centre, opened in September 1995. It is located near the village of Laxton in Nottinghamshire, a rural backwater about 150 miles north of London. The buildings that comprise the museum and its associated educational and research facilities originally formed part of a dilapidated Victorian farmhouse owned by the Smith family. The property functioned as a Christian retreat until the two sons, Stephen and James, made a visit to Yad Vashem in Israel in 1991. Dismayed to discover on their return that there was so little interest in the Holocaust in the United Kingdom, they converted the farmhouse into a Holocaust centre and transformed the grounds into a landscaped commemorative garden. The costs were borne by the family and by private donors. [A fuller account of the early history of Beth Shalom can be found in Smith, 1999.]

The museum is used mainly by groups of students from schools and universities and is also visited by synagogue and church groups. School students are expected to have some knowledge of Nazi Germany and the Holocaust and are given the option of a one or three hour visit, the latter including a talk from a survivor. The Centre is essentially concerned with education and thus, in addition to a conference hall and the museum itself, there are seminar rooms and a library containing over 1,200 books and 15,000 photographs. There is also a mobile exhibition *Another Time, Another Place* ... which is designed to complement the National Curriculum and is available to schools free of charge. Although not open to the general public, Beth Shalom attracts in the region of three hundred visitors a week.

The entrance to the museum is at ground floor level, but virtually all the permanent exhibits are housed in adjoining rooms below ground in an area covering approximately 150 square metres. In descending the stairs the visitor is immediately confronted by a chimney stack rising from the floor. It contains the first names of some of the deportees from Bendzin, a small town in southern Poland chosen to illustrate the way in which individuals and communities were destroyed as part of the attempt to annihilate an entire people. But Bendzin was also chosen to give an insight into the nature and diversity of European Jewry before the Holocaust, a welcome departure from the standard practice of European Holocaust museums which, according to James Young (1999:78), 'begin and end with the destruction of Europe's Jews.' The effect of such a restricted focus is to blind the uninitiated to the 'great vibrancy and richness of Jewish life lost in the Holocaust' (*ibid.*). The community was established in Bendzin during the seventeenth century and by 1931 constituted nearly half its population. The explanatory commentary and accompanying photographs make clear the wide range of social, political, religious and economic activities in which the people were engaged - ordinary people pursuing mundane lives. In an effort to personalise their fate, the visitor is shown photographs of 651 inhabitants (out of the 5,000) who were incarcerated in the town's ghetto and whose ultimate destination was Auschwitz.

Opposite the Bendzin gallery is a substantial display detailing the history of the Jews from the time of the destruction of the Second Temple in 70 CE. In the main, the narrative focuses on the Jews in Europe and the coverage is comprehensive and balanced with reference made to all the well-established landmark events during good times and bad. With regard to the latter, we read of the first Blood Libel (in England in 1144), the expulsions from different European countries, with England again in the vanguard, the Spanish Inquisition, the seventeenth century massacres in the Ukraine, the Russian pogroms and the mass migration they provoked. On the positive side, mention is made of the Golden Ages of Spanish and Polish Jewry and of the rise of a flourishing Yiddish culture in eastern Europe. Recognition is also given to the importance of Jewish emancipation - progressively attained following the French Revolution - and attention is paid to the contribution to the arts, sciences and commerce that Jews were consequently able to make. In this context we learn of the achievements of Einstein, Freud, Kafka, Heine, Rothschild, Mendelssohn and Chagall among others. Plainly, this section of the museum helps to dissolve the popular perception of Jewish history as nothing more than a litany of suffering. It also challenges stereotyped notions of the Jew, for stress is placed on the diversity of the Jewish population in Europe just before the outbreak of war. It is pointed out that 'there were rich and poor, religious and secular, communists and capitalists, professors and labourers.' Particularly gratifying, in view of the widely held assumption that all Jews are wealthy, is the statement that 'the majority (of Jews) lived poor, insignificant and humble lives in the small towns of middle and eastern Europe.'

In covering the history of the Jews there is a brief reference to Judaism. The importance of the Torah and Talmud is highlighted together with Judaism's 'emphasis on moral values and social justice (which) have provided a basis for others to emulate.' However, we are also told that 'the lighting of the Shabbat (Sabbath) candles is very special to Jews wherever they may be.' This statement is not only far from the truth, but unfortunate, in that it once again encourages a perception of Jews as necessarily committed, in some degree, to Judaism. It consequently diminishes the value of the earlier recognition of secular Jews, an ethnic category crucial to an understanding of Nazi racial ideology.

Not surprisingly, a substantial section of the museum is devoted to the history of anti-Semitism, discussed at length under the rubric of 'The Longest Hatred.' An instructive text points an accusing finger at the Christian church noting, among other things, the importance of the charge of deicide and the origins of the legend of the Wandering Jew. Medieval manifestations of anti-Semitism, such as the Blood Libel and the insistence that Jews wear distinctive clothing, are illustrated by a number of wood engravings. This emphasis on the religious origins of anti-Semitism is entirely proper, not just on historical grounds, but as a counterweight to the racist charge (resurrected most recently during the Irving trial) that, by their behaviour, Jews bring anti-Semitism on themselves. Equally, however, visitors ought to be made aware of changes in the Christian attitude towards Judaism that have occurred over the past four decades (Braybrooke, 1998). These changes are not alluded to at Beth Shalom.

The history of racial anti-Semitism, of course, features prominently, with predictable commentaries on the forged *Protocols of the Learned Elders of Zion* and the trial of Alfred Dreyfus. Wagner's anti-Semitism and its impact on Hitler come across clearly and there are also reprints of anti-Semitic caricatures taken from popular periodicals of the time such as *Punch* in the United Kingdom and *Kikeriki* in Austria. The influence of 'race science' on the Nazi *Weltanschauung* is indicated by photographs of racial hygienists at work in pre-war Germany measuring eye and hair colour. One such hygienist, Dr. Sophie Erhardt, is pictured with Roma and Sinti women in 1936.

In a separate gallery the visitor comes face to face with the rise of the Nazi state, written explanations recalling the condition of Germany after the First World War, the Weimar Republic, the founding of the National Socialist German Workers Party and the Munich Putsch of 1923. There are also references to the rampant inflation, Hitler's skilful manipulation of the democratic process and the Reichstag fire. One of the displays considers 'Life in the Third Reich' and deals initially with Hitler's consolidation of power, the corruption of the educational system and the establishment, at Dachau in 1933, of the first concentration camp. The attitude of the churches to the Reich is neatly encapsulated in a statement informing readers that in 1939 the Papal Nuncio sent New Year greetings to Adolf Hitler. The text goes on to record that 'although the Catholic church did not formally associate itself with the Nazi regime, neither did it seek to oppose or offend it.' Naturally, much space is given over to the precarious condition of the Jews in Nazi Germany and to the legislative and other measures that led inexorably to their pariah status. There are references, for example, to the boycott of Jewish businesses, the burning of books by Jewish authors, the dismissal of non-Aryans from the civil service and the Nuremberg Laws. Although there is also a lengthy reference to the targeting of the Jewish community during the *Kristallnacht* pogrom, the cruelty that the Nazis inflicted on other groups at this time is not ignored. There is an account of the compulsory sterilisation programme between 1933 and 1939 which affected 'Aryan' Germans and a report on the sterilisation of hundreds of 'mixed race' teenagers in the Rhineland (the illegitimate children of German women and French soldiers from Senegal.) The situation facing Jehovah's Witnesses - their role as victims of persecution and their resistance to the regime - is discussed briefly and, together with the references to sterilisation go some way towards drawing the distinction between Germans and Nazis. The distinction is reinforced when visitors learn about resistance within Germany. The difficulty of taking effective action is made plain and illustrated by the fate of the most well-known German opponents of Nazism - Dietrich Bonhoeffer and Hans and Sophie Scholl.

The issue of Jewish refugees is tackled in the context of the Evian conference, the Kindertransport and the SS *St. Louis*. The lack of genuine sympathy for the plight of the Jews that prevailed at Evian is commented upon and there is certainly no attempt to disguise what was seen at the time, in some quarters, as the niggardly attitude of the British Government. We learn that 'the ... Empire was said to be over-crowded (and) the option of Palestine, then under British mandate, was not open for discussion.' However, on the other side of the ledger, the United Kingdom's more generous attitude to the Kindertransport (accepting over 10,000 children at the end of the 1930s) is noted along with its preparedness to receive some of the passengers from the *St. Louis*.

The Nazi policy of ghettoization, which followed the German invasion of Poland, is covered very fully. In addition to making use of photographs and written explanations, it is possible to watch, in dimmed light, film footage of ghetto life lasting approximately seven minutes. The scenes of acute privation are overlaid with the voices of Kitty Hart-Moxon, Trudi Levi and others who managed to survive the near-starvation rations, the outbreaks of typhus and the sadism of their captors. One of the accompanying display panels deals with resistance in the ghettos, broadly defined in terms of smuggling in food and information, keeping diaries, educating the young and religious observance. There is also a panel dedicated to Jewish partisan activity and to the armed resistance that broke out in at least twenty ghettos. This emphasis on resistance and especially the uprisings in ghettos other than Warsaw, is a much-needed corrective to the fairly minimal treatment the subject tends to receive in the classroom. That said, students will be left in no doubt as to the ultimate futility of the uprisings. As the caption states, the imbalance of forces 'could do little to stop what had now become inevitable - the total annihilation of European Jewry.'

An account of the Wannsee conference in January 1942, convened to co-ordinate the mass murder of Jews in Nazi-occupied Europe, introduces the section covering 'the Final Solution.' It begins, though, with a reference to the totality of victims of the Nazi terror and focuses in particular on the suffering of the Roma and Sinti. The text reveals that 'over 5,000 of the Lalleri tribe from Austria were deported to the Lodz ghetto (and) were eventually murdered at the Chelmno death camp.' Reference is made to the family camp at Auschwitz and to the medical experiments carried out by Joseph Mengele on the children. Also on show is a glass-encased model of the extermination camp at Treblinka where between July 1942 and April 1943 over 29,000 Roma and Sinti (alongside three-quarters of a million Jews) were murdered. Altogether, we are informed, the death toll among the Roma and Sinti population was somewhere between 200,000 and half a million. This coverage is to be prized because, in common with Jewish resistance, the suffering of the Roma and Sinti is not only an issue significant in its own right, but one that teachers tend to marginalise. We know that their fate had much in common with that of the Jews including the fact that both fell victim to the *Einsatzgruppen* and their local collaborators. The display boards underline these similarities but, at the same time, they fail to provide information about the differences in the attitude and policy of the Nazis towards the two victim groups.

The situation after the war is discussed in terms of the demand for justice and the search for refuge. However, with regard to the former, some significant facts appear to have been omitted. For example, mention is made of the Nuremberg trials but not of any of the trials that took place subsequently, including that of Adolf Eichmann. If it is important to teach students (and others) that murder cannot be committed with impunity, they should know that the hunt for Nazi war criminals did not come to an end in 1946. The display panel also points out that many Nazis escaped justice altogether, often finding a safe haven in South America, but there is no word on the role of the Catholic church in aiding their escape. Such knowledge would seem essential if the depth of hostility that has traditionally marked Christian attitudes towards Jews is to be fully grasped. Many survivors, of course, wanted to go to what was then Palestine but were prevented from doing so by the British Government refusing to lift its immigration restrictions. The harrowing events surrounding the struggle of survivors to enter Palestine, including the shameful episode of the refugee ship 'Exodus' in 1947, are fairly recorded and it is at this point that the museum ends its historical coverage. There is thus no mention of the state of the Jewish world during the half century that has elapsed since the Holocaust. The silence is understandable for such recent history lies outside the museum's remit. None the less, in failing to refer to it, there may be a danger that some visitors (and especially those who in their day-to-day lives never knowingly meet a Jew) will be left with the impression that Hitler was successful in his attempt to destroy the Jewish people. The risk of drawing this conclusion is heightened by the phrase 'total annihilation of European Jewry' that appears on a couple of occasions elsewhere in the museum.

In what seems to be the final gallery, the visitor is able to peruse the condensed biographies of a handful of survivors in which they describe, among other things, rebuilding their lives after the war. However, on leaving the main exhibition area, one notices affixed to the wall, a series of portraits and brief citations about a number of people who rescued Jews. Famed individuals (such as Wallenberg, Schindler and Pastor Andre Trocme) are featured and, as expected, there is a reference to the role of the Danes. Some less well-rehearsed stories of rescue are also told, such as that of the mayor of Cernauti in Romania who issued special exemption passes and is thought to have saved thousands of Jews from deportation. While the museum designers obviously intended to salute the courage and humanity of these 'righteous gentiles,' the fact that they are, in a sense, set apart from the main exhibits might suggest to some visitors that their role in the Holocaust was peripheral. In the greater scheme of things, of course, their role was indeed peripheral, for there were far too few of them. However, in terms of their potential to act as role models for future generations their importance cannot be over-stated and for this reason it is regrettable that their heroism is not celebrated more prominently and at an earlier stage in the narrative.

Despite its few shortcomings, there can be no doubt that secondary school students are able to derive considerable benefit from an organised visit to Beth Shalom. One teacher of religious education, a few years ago, recorded the following comments from his class of 13- and 14-year-olds.

> The talk Mr. Katz gave us really touched my heart and I felt great sorrow for what he had been through.

What people went through - the amount of emotion, fear and pain was incredible.
I did not really understand the Holocaust before I went to Beth Shalom.

It helped me to learn a lot more than school lessons.

(Brown, 1999:9)

These observations and others from pupils of a similar age that regularly
appear in the Centre's newsletter *Perspective*, effectively answer those who
question whether it is 'possible to recall with any genuine feeling an event that is
outside both our experience and our time' (Sewell , 1999).

THE HOLOCAUST EDUCATION AND MEMORIAL CENTRE OF TORONTO
(UNITED JEWISH APPEAL FEDERATION)

Beginnings

In the late 1970s and early 1980s, when the cocoon of forgetting that had
surrounded the Holocaust was beginning to rupture, two survivors who had settled
in Toronto donated a significant sum of money to establish a local Holocaust
Memorial Centre.[†] It was to be built on a large multi-site tract of land in the north
of the city and an architect and conceptual designer were contracted to plan the
space and the permanent exhibit. They were presented with 1,700 square feet and
informed that the guiding consideration of any design should be a commitment to
public education about the Holocaust. To signal this commitment, the complex was
to be named the Holocaust Education and Memorial Centre of Toronto and would
comprise a memorial museum and a resource and administrative centre.

Working in tandem, the architect and designer fashioned a circular space
and created a multi-dimensional exhibit that tells the story of the Holocaust in three
segments; life before, during and after the Holocaust. Because the space set aside
was quite small, it was anticipated that it would not function successfully as a
traditional walk-through museum. Rather, an attempt would be made to describe

---

[†] Although private donations were the generating impulse for the creation of the Centre, its
ongoing administration and programming was funded from the outset by the United Jewish
Appeal Federation of Greater Toronto, the central communal organisation in the city.
Through the Council of Jewish Federations located in New York, the Toronto federation is
connected to over 800 Jewish communities across North America.

the events surrounding the Holocaust on a number of levels simultaneously - by architectural design, by music and by a series of photographic images. These three experiential effects - spacial, aural and visual - were to help prepare visitors affectively for the unfolding of the Holocaust narrative.

The Memorial Museum

Visitors are greeted at the portal to the museum by an oversized set of doors. Each is covered with a sheet of bronze sculpted in a three-dimensional design to depict the Hebrew letter 'shin'. Taken together the letters are read as 'shesh,' the number six and represent the six million Jews who were murdered. One of the letters is smaller than the other and draws attention to the million or so Jewish children who perished. Side by side, the letters also depict a six armed candelabra, a variation on the menorah, a Jewish artefact used in religious observances to foster historical memory. Around the candelabra are three-dimensional curved lines that look like smoke rising to the heavens and some of the lines can be 'read' to represent floating images of people carried aloft by the rising smoke. The doors, rich in symbolism, act as both a metaphorical and a literal boundary to the museum. When visitors step beyond them they can sense that they are entering another world - one filled with deep significance. It is immediately noticeable that the museum is dark. The atmosphere, created by special lighting, is intended to signal entry to a no man's land - one bereft of light. The way forward leads to the first part of the exhibit; a gallery displaying photographs of prominent Jews and aspects of Jewish life in central and eastern Europe before the Holocaust.

Life before the Holocaust

The photographs are illuminated from behind by low wattage bulbs and line both walls of the passageway. One side presents an array of illustrious figures; politicians, artists, businessmen and humanitarians. Students may have heard of some of them but not been aware of their Jewish identity. They include Sigmund Freud, Benjamin Disraeli, Sara Bernhardt, Albert Einstein, Gustav Mahler, Karl Marx and Rosa Luxemberg. While the purpose of these photographs is presumably to give students some notion of the Jewish contribution to western civilisation, they may also prompt them to think about what was lost to that civilisation as a result of the Holocaust.

On the other side of the passageway are photographs and accompanying commentaries on the pre-war East European Jewish community and family life of the *shtetl* (small town or village). The pictures present a plethora of vignettes depicting everyday events such as weddings and other social gatherings and people working, studying and engaging in various leisure pursuits. As with Beth Shalom, an attempt is made to counter the falsehood of ubiquitous Jewish opulence by pointing out that the shtetls were 'desperately poor.' There is also a useful, albeit implicit, warning against associating anti-Semitism with Germany alone, for the text states that between 1919 and 1921 pogroms cost at least 20,000 lives in the Ukraine. Additionally, the display panel contains features on political milestones in modern Jewish history such as the formation of the Bund and the early days of Zionism. There are, however, no references to Jewish life prior to the Enlightenment. This omission is understandable in view of the limited space available, but unfortunate in so far as it denies students (and others) an opportunity to see the Holocaust in historical perspective.

At the end of the passageway is an arch made of roughly hewn blocks of stone. It is meant to cause visitors to feel somewhat crowded as they pass through it, symbolizing the cramped conditions of the ghetto. Having crossed the stone threshold, visitors enter a 60 seat theatre.

'Images'

On the screen before them flash a number of images dissolving into one another. They are accompanied by a vocal chorus. The music is haunting and reminiscent of a Gregorian chant and the sound and imagery together heighten the feeling of being in a vanished world. Some of the images are of ordinary Jewish people in pre-war Europe engaged in mundane activities. Others are representations of the Holocaust itself. Among them are pictures of mass graves, people being herded into trains, the infamous clock tower of Auschwitz-Birkenau, piles of naked corpses and, most horrifically, murdered babies. The images appear one by one on the screen in no particular order and the viewer is forced to confront the reality that the piles of bodies could have contained the ordinary individuals they saw a moment earlier - people, seemingly, much like themselves. The purpose of the juxtaposition of normality and horror is to diminish the distance between victim and viewer.

The Holocaust

The 'Images' presentation is followed by a documentary slide show that constitutes the intellectual heart of the exhibit. Lasting almost thirty minutes, it delineates the events of the Holocaust using nearly a thousand photographs acquired from various archives around the world. The narration begins with an explanation of the historical roots of anti-Semitism and traces its evolution to the rise of Nazism. It depicts the successive stages leading from the Weimar Republic to the 'Final Solution' and goes on to cover the liberation and its aftermath. All the major developments are referred to; questions are asked about the role of the Church and attention is drawn to the post-war trials and their impact on human rights. In respect of the latter, the narrative is highly critical of the Canadian Government's attitude towards the admission of Jewish refugees both before the war and in the immediate post-war years. The final utterance, 'A warning,' signifies that the purpose of the documentary is to inspire vigilance in order to safeguard human rights.

The audio-visual presentation was originally put together in the mid-1980s and despite some recent changes remains essentially unchanged. It makes complicated historical material readily accessible to a lay audience. It is unflinching in its depiction of the Final Solution but does not indulge in empty shock value. And although it threads strands of hope through the narrative by noting acts of resistance and heroism, it does not slip into sentimentality or shallow optimism. The narrative is, however, marred by some troubling omissions. For example, there is no mention of secular Jews. We have referred on a number of occasions to the consequences of this distortion; namely, a tendency to overstate the role of religious identity in the Holocaust. In our view, the audio-visual presentation further contributes to this misunderstanding by alleging that Hitler was particularly keen to kill children because they would otherwise help to perpetuate Judaism. A further omission relates to the slides showing some of the grotesque caricatures of Jews that have scarred the last thousand years of European history. The accompanying commentary fails to point out clearly that they *are* caricatures and may thus leave some students with the impression that the murdered Jews were indeed as repulsive and demonic as the Nazis claimed. Finally, we note the minimal number of references in the presentation to the Nazis' persecution of non-Jews.

Artefacts

The display cases contain artefacts from the Nazi period including a canister of Zyklon B gas, a concentration camp uniform, Jewish passports and several identity badges including the yellow star that Jews were forced to wear in most of occupied Europe. There is also a Torah scroll that was rescued during *Kristallnacht* by a priest. He subsequently gave it to a Jewish chaplain in the Canadian army who donated it to the Centre. Other artefacts include a pair of children's shoes, a drinking cup and eating bowl used in one of the camps and an ivory necklace plundered from Riga. Also on view is a ceremonial Nazi dagger, although it is not clear what educational purpose it is intended to serve as far as understanding the Holocaust is concerned.

Hall of Memories and the Research and Resources Wall

In the centre of the museum, opposite the display of artefacts, is a walled-off circular space - the Hall of Memories. The architect envisioned this area as a place where the visitor could come after learning about the Holocaust and take a moment to reflect. In order to suggest symbolically that through memory and reflection there is hope, the circular hall is bathed in dazzling light. To add to the effect, the walls are covered with white glazed clay tiles. They allude to the biblical notion of 'from dust to dust' and underscore the fact that each of the six million deaths represented an individual's life returned to the earth. Many of the tiles have been inscribed with the name of a victim.

Close to the Hall of Memories is the Research and the Resource wall. It contains a number of large flip-panel displays that deal in considerable depth with a host of issues relevant to the Holocaust and its aftermath, including racism in present-day Canada.

Life after the Holocaust

The ascending passageway leading to the exit contains illuminated photographic displays relating to developments in the Jewish world since the Holocaust. In contrast to Beth Shalom, which ends its historical coverage with survivors arriving in what was to become Israel, the Toronto museum depicts events in Israel after 1948. It presents images of both religious and secular life. There are, in addition, representations of post-war Jewish communities in various parts of the diaspora, including the United States, Romania, Morocco, South Africa and Canada. There is thus little prospect of anyone leaving the museum under the misapprehension that the Nazis realised their aim of destroying the Jewish people. These pictures, together with those of prominent rescuers, are meant to end the visit on a hopeful note. The photographs of Canadians involved in the liberation of Europe are likely to help achieve this goal.

The last illuminated panel highlights various inspirational texts, including quotations from the Bible and also features poetry and reflections from well-known survivors such as Elie Wiesel and Primo Levi.

Docents - Survivor Speakers - School Tours

Although the museum was designed to enable visitors to experience the exhibit without the need for a docent-led tour, groups can arrange one and can also hear a survivor speak. There are over sixty such speakers who volunteer their services. Although many groups and individuals visit the Centre, it caters mainly for secondary schools. Approximately 25,000 students from all over Ontario (and sometimes from Quebec and the United States), make the trip each year. A school visit usually lasts two hours. After a half hour guided tour, students view the audio-visual presentation and follow it with an hour spent listening to a survivor recount his or her Holocaust experience. They are then encouraged to ask questions or discuss their response to the visit.

The impact that survivors have on students can be gauged from the following representative extracts from four letters originally sent to one of the speakers, the late Robert Engel. They come from Grade 11 students.

> Before arriving at the Holocaust centre, we, as a class, watched *Schindler's List* to prepare us. The movie was horrifically realistic, yet could not prepare us for your story. Your story was compelling and moving ... Sir, you really touched me then; that is one day of my life that I will never forget. When you told us about your liberators being Canadian I couldn't help but blush and feel an overwhelming sense of national pride.

> I learnt more yesterday from what you told us than what any teacher in any classroom could ever teach. The film clip was really informative, but sad, and the objects in the glass case really made me see reality. But your story is what really made me think.

> Your experience has touched me and made me think of what we have and what we take for granted.

> You taught something I will treasure throughout my ... life; that people can make a difference, and when you do reach out to someone in their time of need, or stand up for them, or whatever you do, it is one of the most satisfying feelings in the world.

Critique

We have already articulated some of our reservations about the museum and the audio-visual presentation in particular. We drew attention to the lack of serious concern it gives to the victimization of non-Jewish groups. Their suffering is referred to in detail in the Research and Resources section, but many visitors may not feel inclined to undertake the necessary reading. As a result, the rather sketchy treatment of this topic in the presentation may leave some visitors with the impression that Jews were the only group targeted in earnest by the Nazis.

A similar criticism concerns equitable gender representation. In the section providing information about the contribution that Jews have made to European civilisation, very few women are included. The examples provided of famous Jewish philosophers, psychoanalysts and artists are almost entirely male. Karl Marx, Sigmund Freud and Amedeo Modigliani feature prominently, but why not Hannah Arendt, Anna Freud, or Charlotte Salomon? Out of the 39 notables on display, 36 are men. For a museum concerned with the abuse of human rights, this is clearly a missed opportunity.

The last reservation we have concerns the age appropriateness of the audio-visual presentation. Due to the demand for historical accuracy, many of the slides are graphically disturbing. We have no problem with the suitability of this material for adults and older secondary school students, but the Centre is often visited by children from middle and elementary schools. We question whether the presentation, in its current form, is sufficiently sensitive to the needs of the youngest age-groups.

In spite of these misgivings we are confident, not least because of the student reaction we have cited, that the museum serves as a valuable learning resource for many schools in the Toronto area and further afield.

Chapter 9

Teaching the Holocaust to Young Children

We argued at the beginning of Chapter 2 that as schools reflect and reproduce the dominant culture, the extent to which the Holocaust is represented in the curriculum will depend on its salience in the wider society. Whether the Holocaust will be taught in the primary school, however, is contingent upon an additional factor and that is the prevailing conception of childhood in contemporary educational discourse. Until recently, the majority of primary school teachers in the United Kingdom were assumed to subscribe to a set of beliefs about child development that would not have been conducive to their teaching the Holocaust or any other topic exposing the less wholesome side of human existence. Robin Alexander (1984) has dubbed these beliefs 'primary ideology.' They constitute a form of pedagogic folklore which, *inter alia*, views childhood as an age of innocence and recognises that infants in particular, while capable of unacceptable behaviour, remain free from malicious intent. [Alexander's claim that teachers accept this Rousseauesque view of the child's moral purity was determined, in part, by Ronald King's (1978) observational study of three infant schools in the south of England]. Teachers of Junior school children (aged between 7 and 11) might have been expected to show rather less concern with protecting the naive innocence of their pupils, but in the mid-1980s, they too, apparently, drew the line at controversial issues (Ross, 1984).

A second facet of primary ideology identified by Alexander relates to Piaget's work on cognitive development and its influence on the curriculum. As is well known, Piaget stressed the intellectual limitations of young children and, in particular, their inability to think in the abstract. In so far as the Holocaust is seen to demand an understanding of fairly sophisticated concepts, the impact of Piagetian theory on primary school teachers will therefore militate against their engagement with the subject. Among the ideas that immature minds may have difficulty assimilating is that of Jews as an ethnic group as opposed to a religious one. This notion is, of course, key to an understanding of Nazi racial ideology. Piaget's (1932) work on moral development suggests that young children may also have problems with the whole idea of condemning people to death on account of their ethnicity rather than because of anything they have done.

Today, these theoretical constraints on the teaching of controversial or sensitive issues are treated with considerable scepticism. We have abundant evidence that young children's innocence has been greatly exaggerated in relation to a host of 'political' issues and not least in relation to their understanding of racism (see, for example, Milner, 1983; Department of Education and Science, 1985). We also have considerable evidence that children are far more able intellectually than was previously thought. Over the past quarter of a century, Piaget's account of cognitive development has frequently been tested and found wanting (e.g. Donaldson, 1978; Dunn, 1988; Wood, 1998) and the views of the Russian psychologist Lev Vygotsky (1956) on the value of adult instruction are now in vogue. Teachers have consequently been urged to raise their expectations of children's abilities in all areas of the curriculum. In effect, they have been encouraged to side with Piaget's critics and adopt a more positive view of the young child's intellectual reach. In the light of this theoretical shift, it would not be surprising to find an increasing number of primary schools teaching the Holocaust; indeed, it has recently been argued that the subject may be suitable for children of kindergarten age (Sepinwall, 1999).

According to Samuel Totten (1999), Holocaust education, when applied to the teaching of very young children, is often a misnomer, for it implies nothing more than an attempt to develop personal qualities like tolerance and respect for difference, or social skills such as peaceful conflict resolution. It does not involve teaching the history of the Holocaust *per se.* However, where children between the ages of five and nine *are* taught aspects of this history and where they may also come into contact with Holocaust survivors, Totten objects strongly. He does so for three reasons.

> First, the history is far too complex for young children to understand. ... Second, without a fairly solid understanding of the (critical) concepts it is difficult for anyone to truly understand why and how the Holocaust unfolded. Third, it is simply and profoundly inappropriate to introduce, let alone immerse such young children (in) the various horrors of the Holocaust.
>
> (Totten, 1999:38)

Totten expresses particular distaste for books on the Holocaust produced for young children. He draws attention to Sepinwall's description of some of them.

> They may tell stories of strained and lost relationships, or of hidden children and their rescuers, or they may deal more specifically with the Holocaust by describing the lives of those forced into concentration camps, of families separated and then reunited, or of children facing life as survivors after the Holocaust. Still other books encourage children to see the Holocaust in the context of historic anti-Semitism and to remember the victims of the Holocaust.
>
> (Sepinwall, 1999:7)

In connection with these remarks, Totten asks, 'without contextualisation, how will such young students even begin to understand why the children were in hiding, in need of rescue or separated from their families' (p. 38). His major concern, however, is with books that 'provide graphic details of the horrors,' claiming that 'such information could result in 'nightmares and other psychological distress' (p. 37). Karen Shawn (1999:423) points to 'a discernible (and disturbing) trend toward publishing Holocaust literature for ever-younger primary grade students' and, consistent with Totten's fears, claims that 'many of these works are more graphic and depressing than those aimed at middle and high school students.' She goes on to suggest 'that the details of the Final Solution be taught only in high school, and that no book about the Holocaust, even the simplest, be offered to students before second grade' (p. 424).

The debate over whether to teach the Holocaust in the primary or elementary school seems more finely balanced in relation to children above the age of nine. There would appear to be no consensus, for example, over the extent to which such children are able to cope emotionally with the topic's more gruesome aspects. Margie Marmur, an experienced Vice-Principal of an inner city school in Toronto, is keen to play down the graphic detail.

> We certainly talk about the fact that there were concentration camps and the purpose of a concentration camp. We don't spend a lot of time talking about what it looked like and not a lot of time exposing kids to pictures, although in elementary school we do use photographs.
> I think our purpose in elementary education is not to terrify the children, not to cause them to be afraid and alarmed, but rather to look at the behaviour of people and problem-solving in conflict situations. We don't spend a lot of time talking about the horror. We acknowledge that it was an awful thing ... and look at how people coped.

A somewhat different account emerged in a comparatively recent study by Maitles and Cowan (1999) in Scotland, the only empirical research we have come across on teaching the Holocaust in the primary school.

An Empirical Study

Maitles and Cowan's investigation was small-scale, involving semi-structured interviews with just five teachers, all of whom were female and worked in non-denominational schools. Their pupils were aged between 9 and 11. The teachers were selected for a number of reasons but mainly, it seems, because they had indicated in a questionnaire, sent randomly to 40 primary schools in the Strathclyde region, that they include the Holocaust in the curriculum and would be willing to participate in an in-depth interview.

All five teachers integrated the Holocaust into one of three areas; namely, Understanding the Past, Religious and Moral Education, and Personal and Social

Development. The story of Anne Frank played a prominent part in their teaching and for this purpose they all regularly used the instructional pack *Into Hiding* (Rendell, 1987) They also taught the Holocaust through art and craft activities and through role play. The latter was said to be successful (cf. Dawidowicz), for it 'brought the topic to life in a personal way.' All the teachers showed videos which were mainly about the life of Anne Frank, but also included extracts from Leni Riefenstahl's *Triumph of the Will.* Survivors addressed the children and apparently made a useful contribution. '(Teachers) commented positively on the value of these speakers in helping pupils understand that the Holocaust was real and not just another story (p. 268).'

As we have implied, the most contentious aspect of teaching the Holocaust in the primary school relates to the way in which systematic murder is handled. *Into Hiding* makes reference to the concentration camp at Bergen-Belsen and to the extermination camp at Auschwitz, but in the space of a few short paragraphs, it does not go into detail. Four of the five teachers found this superficial coverage unsatisfactory and all of them, for different reasons, ended up giving their pupils considerably more information. Many pupils had, in fact, acquired knowledge of the camps before they were discussed in class where, according to Maitles and Cowan, there was 'no evidence to suggest that teachers had any difficulty in presenting this part of the topic ...' (p. 269). In view of what was said earlier about childhood innocence, their observation is an interesting one. However, it is not known whether the teachers also dealt with the *Einsatzgruppen*, a topic that young children might respond to with rather less equanimity.

In common with history staff in English secondary schools (see Chapter 5), the teachers appeared to use the Holocaust as a vehicle for combating racism in general rather than anti-Semitism in particular. Maitles and Cowan pass no judgment on this tendency; nor do they comment on any problems the teachers encountered (other than 'a lack of history books, posters and pictures' suitable for primary aged pupils). On the contrary, they maintain that for both teachers and pupils, learning about the Holocaust was a rewarding experience. As they put it: '(The) survey suggests that, with the appropriate methodology, the Holocaust is a successful, stimulating area of study for pupils of primary 5 (aged 9 years) upwards. Once they have done so, teachers are keen to teach the Holocaust again' (p. 270). Unfortunately, the researchers did not interview the pupils and so it is not possible to ascertain, with any degree of confidence, what they learnt and how, if at all, they may have benefited from their exposure to the Holocaust. Bearing in mind the misconceptions and lacunae in the knowledge of the Holocaust revealed by English 14- and 15-year-olds (discussed in Chapter 6), we fear that much younger children may emerge from their introduction to the subject with a limited and distorted understanding. Our fear is based partly on two studies of primary school children's conceptions of Jewish culture and identity published in England during the 1990s (Short, 1991a; Short and Carrington, 1995).

Young Children's Understanding of Jewish Culture and Identity

The research involved interviews with two groups of children, one aged 8 and 9; the other 10 and 11. There were 130 in total. All the younger children attended a socially-mixed, non-denominational school in an area of south-east England adjacent to a substantial Jewish community. The older children were drawn from four schools; one in the north-east of England and three in the south-east. The northern school had a working-class catchment and was located within a few miles of both a mainstream Jewish community and a Chassidic (ultra-orthodox) one. The southern schools were predominantly middle-class and rather closer to mainstream Jewish communities. There is no suggestion that the children were representative of their respective age groups, for one would expect responses to the interviews to vary as a function of many factors including geographical location, ethnic composition of the school and religious affiliation of the pupils. Virtually all the children in this study were white and nominally Christian. Nonetheless, they may be considered sufficiently representative to suggest some of the problems, as well as the possibilities, of teaching the Holocaust in the primary school.

8- and 9-year-olds

At an early stage in the interview, the children were asked if they had ever heard the word 'Jew' or 'Jewish.' Among those answering in the affirmative, some clearly had no idea what the word referred to.

> Claire: (8 years, 6 months) I think so, once. I heard someone say it.
>
> Michael: (8:7) Yes. Is it a language?
>
> Pamela: (9:1) Yes. In a book I think. Was Jews a name?
>
> Paul: (8:6) I heard it in Assembly once.
>
> *Interviewer*: Can you remember what was said?
>
> Paul: No.

Among those who did possess a rudimentary concept of a Jew, there was still a fair amount of confusion. A number of children, for instance, saw Jews as necessarily alien and the notion of a British Jew seemed incomprehensible to some of them.

Interviewer: Have you ever heard the word 'Jewish'?

Peter: Yes.

Interviewer: What have you heard?

Peter: People from Jerusalem. They're Jewish.

Interviewer: So, if you are born in England, can you be Jewish?

Peter: Yes, if you go to Jerusalem for a long time.

Thinking along similar lines, Matthew (9:2) maintained that we do have Jewish people in England because 'they could come here for a holiday.' Asked if it was possible for someone Jewish to be born in England, he said it was not.

Although Alex (8:7) perceived Jews as foreign, it is not clear whether this was because he had only ever encountered the ultra-orthodox (with their distinctive appearance) or because he confused Jews with Sikhs.

> *Interviewer*: If you could choose to be Christian or Jewish, which would you prefer or are you not bothered?
>
> Alex: Christian, because Jewish people are sort of foreign - all funny ways.
>
> *Interviewer*: So you think Jewish people in this country are foreign do you?
>
> Alex: Yes.
>
> *Interviewer*: Why do you think that?
>
> Alex: Because when you look at them, they got sort of a funny beard and they got something round their head and (it) just doesn't look like a British person.

The comments made by these boys are noteworthy in the light of Grugeon and Woods' (1990) observations on a project on Judaism carried out in England by a group of 7- and 8-year-olds. After interviewing the children, the researchers concluded that 'there was a general feeling that Jews were not English.'

It would appear from the comments cited above that many 8- and 9-year-olds have no concept, or virtually no concept, of a Jew. One wonders, therefore, what the children in the Maitles and Cowan study learnt from their lessons on the Holocaust, for they were only one year older. It certainly seems reasonable to conclude that to have learnt anything worthwhile they would require much preparatory work on the nature of Jewish identity. That said, it is not known whether the generality of children of this age are capable of benefiting from such preparatory work (but see below).

10- and 11-year-olds

It was the 10- and 11-year-olds in just one of the schools in south-east England who were questioned about the nature of Jewish identity. Unlike the younger children attending the same school, they seemed well acquainted with the 'biological' definition that was so central to Nazi ideology. They were also aware of the distinction between racial and cultural definitions of Jewishness. Their understanding was, perhaps, due in part to the fact that they had been taught the previous year by a woman who was the daughter of a Jewish mother (who had fled Nazi Germany) and a non-Jewish father. The teacher had spoken at length to the class about her mother's pre-war experiences and of her own lack of commitment to Judaism.

Having explored with the children their knowledge of different religions and of Judaism in particular, they were asked what they knew about Jewish people. The comments of Tanita and John (interviewed together) are typical and leave no doubt that *some* children of this age, and perhaps the majority, are able to understand Jewishness as a racial as well as a religious identity.

> Tanita: Our last teacher used to tell us something because she was half-Jewish. She was Jewish by 'race', not religion.
>
> *Interviewer*: What does that mean?
>
> Tanita: She was born Jewish, but she didn't take it into her religion. She didn't go to the religious things.
>
> *Interviewer*: If someone is born Jewish and wants to become a Christian, will they stop being Jewish?
>
> Tanita: No, I don't think so. They will always be Jewish, but they can act like a Christian.
>
> John: (11:0) You're still partly Jewish.
>
> *Interviewer*: What do you mean?
>
> John: Your parents are. You're Jewish by blood, but you make yourself think that you're not.
>
> *Interviewer*: If, when you are born, your parents are Christian, can you later become Jewish?
>
> John: Yes, but you would still, in your blood, be a Christian.

As was pointed out in Chapter 4, if Holocaust education is to be undertaken successfully we need to know more about children's thinking than whether they are able to distinguish racial from religious definitions of Jewishness. We also need to know how they perceive Judaism and, in particular, its relationship to Christianity. From this standpoint, one of the more common misconceptions to emerge from interviews with the 10- and 11-year-olds (seen in pairs in all four schools) was that Jews and Christians worship different gods. Some children thought that Jews worshipped quite a few.

Interviewer: Do Jews believe in the same God as Christians?

Wayne (10:3): No.

Interviewer: Which God do they believe in then?

Wayne: Silly Gods. They pray to their own God. They can pray to the Christian God if they want to, but some of them don't.

Martin (10:7) (Jews pray to) different gods.

Interviewer: So, which God do Christians pray to and which do Jews pray to?

Martin: Christians pray to Jesus; not sure about Jews.

Simon; (10:11): I've been past a synagogue down Washington Lane. It's a crematorium and these people are buried under the church with all the gods.

For reasons that were explored in Chapter 4, the children were also questioned about their knowledge of Jesus. Well over half the sample did not know that he was a Jew and 14 per cent were prepared to blame the Jews, without qualification, for his death. Clearly, such 'knowledge' is not helpful to children conceptualising Nazism as an unmitigated evil. To tap their familiarity with anti-Semitic stereotypes, the children were also asked if they had ever heard anything unkind said about Jews. [As with similar research reported in an earlier chapter, the children were first invited to say whether they had heard anything unkind about Christians.] It transpired that many of them were cognisant of an unsavoury association of Jews with money.

Wendy: If you pick up a penny you're a Jew.

Interviewer: What does that mean?

Wendy: If you're a Christian and you pick up a penny, they call you a Jew.

Interviewer: Why do people say that?

Wendy: Because the Jews do that.

Interviewer: Have you ever heard anyone say anything nasty or unkind about Jews?

Nicola: Yes. They go for all the money; every piece of money they can get.

Interviewer: Where did you hear this?

Nicola: Around the school.

We revealed in Chapter 4 that some 13- and 14-year-olds subscribed to outlandish notions of Judaism which, in common with unflattering stereotypes of Jews, might inhibit an appropriate response to the Holocaust. Not surprisingly, younger children articulated some equally outlandish notions involving, in a few instances, the sort of ignorance that could invite contempt for Jews. The following comments, made in response to the question: 'What do you know about the Jewish religion?', are representative.

> They have Passover. It's when angels come over killing every baby boy and you have to put blood on your door so that they don't come.

> When they die, my dad said, they keep their jewellery in their grave.

Resources for Teaching the Holocaust to Young Children

In order to illustrate the difficulties of teaching the Holocaust to young children, we consider in this section some of the resources designed for use in the primary school. We begin by looking at the teaching pack produced by the Anne Frank Educational Trust (1996) which has been purchased by over 4,500 schools. Although mainly concerned to provide ideas for commemorating Anne Frank's birthday, the pack also includes a useful chronology of the Frank family, extracts from the diary, an annotated bibliography of Holocaust literature suitable for a young readership and a number of monochrome photographs to complement the narrative. Most of the suggested activities are directed at teachers of 7- to 11-year-olds and have the twin purpose of providing information about the life of Anne Frank and assisting children to become more tolerant and more appreciative of the benefits of living in a democratic society. For our purposes, we will focus on the one activity recommended for 5- to 7-year-olds. It is suggested that schools hold an assembly for children in this age group with the aim of introducing them 'to Anne Frank as someone who was special and to explore and celebrate friendship as a special relationship.' A story is to be read to the children which starts as follows:

> There once lived a girl called Anne Frank. She was born in the city of Frankfurt in Germany on 12 June 1929. In that country there were people who hated Jews. They were called Nazis. Four years after Anne Frank was born, the Nazis and their leader

Adolf Hitler became the most powerful people in the land. Anne Frank and her family were Jews and so they knew that soon their lives would be in danger. They moved to another country called Holland where they could feel safer.

In view of the evidence we have produced showing that 8- and 9-year-olds have almost no conception of a Jew, one wonders what 5- and 6-year-olds will make of this story. One wonders too how a teacher would respond if a child, quite reasonably, were to ask, 'What is a Jew and why did the Nazis not like them?' To discuss with young children the nature and value of friendship (and to include in the discussion references to inanimate 'friends' such as diaries) is perfectly sensible, but to do so in the context of Anne Frank seems to us to complicate the issue unnecessarily.

A subsequent resource published by the Anne Frank Educational Trust (2000) suffers from the same problem. It is again concerned with citizenship but this time introduces Anne Frank to children aged between 7 and 11.

> The Frank family were middle-class German Jews who enjoyed a comfortable lifestyle among the well-established communities of Frankfurt. Jews, who had lived in the city since the Middle Ages, constituted about 5.5% of the population. They were able to maintain their traditions in a city where the law had given them equal rights at the beginning of the 19th century.

Teachers are advised that 'a discussion of what (Anne Frank) was deprived of as a Jew in hiding should lead to a discussion on human rights.' Once more, however, we have to ask what the youngest children (the 7- and 8-year-olds) are likely to make of this recommended activity in so far as it requires them to possess a concept of a Jew.

Some literature on the Holocaust recommended for children of elementary school age (Goldberg, 1996) confronts the vexed issue of Jewish identity by equating it with religious conviction. Such an approach is evident in the well-known and highly recommended novella *Friedrich* (Richter, 1987). It has sold in excess of two million copies since its publication in 1961 and tells the story of two boys, one Jewish, the other 'Aryan' who were born within a week of each other in 1925. Every one of the Jewish characters in the book (including the anti-Semitic grandfather's colleague at work) is an observant Jew and as one expression of the religious dimension, the narrator details preparations for a Friday night (Sabbath) meal at the Schneider household:

> Frau Schneider spread a white cloth over the table, a cloth of such radiant white that it shone in the dim room. From the cupboard she took two candlesticks with new candles in them. From the kitchen she fetched two small home-made loaves of bread. These two loaves she placed on the table between the candlesticks and Herr Schneider's place.
> ... A moment later he entered the living room dressed in a dark suit and wearing a tiny embroidered (skull) cap. Friedrich went to meet his father. Herr Schneider laid a hand on his head and said, 'May God make thee as Ephraim and

Manasseh. May the Lord bless thee and keep thee: may the Lord cause his countenance to shine upon thee, and be gracious unto thee. May the Lord lift up his countenance towards thee and give thee peace.' Then he opened the prayer book and read something to his wife in Hebrew (pp. 17-18).

There are other occasions in the book when the reader is led to conclude that Jews, by definition, are religious. The Schneider family's doctor, for instance, is referred to as 'a middle-aged man in a dark suit (with a) yumulka (skull cap) on his head.' A whole chapter is given over to Friedrich's bar mitzvah and even the guest speaker at the *Jungvolk* meeting illustrates the threat that Jews allegedly pose to Germany by discussing at length the ritual slaughter of animals.

Concluding Comment

In this concluding section we discuss whether it is possible to teach the Holocaust meaningfully in the primary school and, in so far as it is possible, whether it should be undertaken. We have argued that no useful work can be done on the Holocaust if children have no concept of Jewishness as a racial classification and that on the basis of our own research, we suspect that many, and perhaps most children in the lower primary school (below the age of 9), will lack this concept in the absence of substantial preparatory work. For those a little older, the uncertainty persists. Some of the teachers in the Maitles and Cowan study worked with 9- to 10-year-olds and reported no difficulties, but we note that they were not asked directly about any difficulties they may have had and that none of the children were interviewed to assess their understanding of the topic. It seems likely, however, that the majority of children above the age of ten do have the ability to conceptualise Jews as a racial or ethnic group. In drawing a line at this age we do not mean to imply that nothing of value can be achieved with younger children that is of relevance to the Holocaust. Bruner's (1960:33) much quoted dictum that 'any subject can be taught effectively in some intellectually honest form to any child at any stage of development' suggests otherwise. In the light of this claim we would advocate, along with Totten (*op. cit.*), that teachers of young children spend time on matters relating to prejudice and social justice rather than on the Holocaust itself (see, for example, Short and Carrington, 1991; Siraj-Blatchford, 1994).

Whether the Holocaust should be taught in the upper reaches of the primary school depends, in part, on whether local secondary schools are obliged to teach it. In countries such as Scotland where this is not the case, the argument for covering the topic in the primary school is a powerful one, for the alternative would be to risk students leaving school with no awareness of it at all. For Maitles and Cowan, however, there are strong grounds for primary schools engaging with the Holocaust regardless of whether it is taught at secondary level. Their reasoning is based partly on the fact that the event lends itself to cross-curricular study which, in their view, can be achieved more easily in the primary than in the secondary school because the former is not constrained by a departmental structure. They also believe that as primary school teachers have more control over their day-to-day planning, they are better able to respond to the needs of their pupils. They can, for example, extend lessons in a way that is denied to their secondary colleagues. Furthermore, primary school teachers develop a closer relationship with their pupils and are thus better placed to foster classroom discussion and encourage the more diffident to participate.

Where the Holocaust is taught at secondary level, the main argument against introducing it to a younger age group was summed up by a Canadian teacher whose views we reported in Chapter 5. Essentially, he referred to what might be termed 'Holocaust fatigue'; the notion that if students have had too much exposure to the subject prior to learning about it, again, as part of a history course, the boredom factor may set in with the result that students take it less seriously than they should and learn less than they otherwise might.

Endnote

Reflecting on the current state of Holocaust education in the United Kingdom and Canada, we have been struck by the relative dearth of literature underpinned by research. Although limited in quantity, we have no doubt that much of this literature has important implications for the classroom and should therefore be known to all who teach the Holocaust in schools. To help achieve this goal, we have drawn attention to a number of empirical studies and have commented at length on their practical relevance. However, we are well aware of the shortcomings of the studies, and in this brief epilogue, offer a critique of the work we have cited before considering the future direction of research in the field of Holocaust education.

To illustrate the issues that concern us, we focus initially on our examination of teachers' attitudes and practices described in Chapter 5. We have to admit that not only were the samples involved relatively small and opportunistic, but that the research was conducted in regions of the United Kingdom and Canada that cannot be seen as representative of either. The vast majority of schools were located in metropolitan centres with a substantial ethnic minority population. While we do not think it likely, we recognise that the results might have been very different had we embarked upon the work elsewhere and particularly in less urbanised and less cosmopolitan areas. Again, if we look at the study dealing with the impact of Holocaust education on adolescents' understanding of citizenship (discussed in Chapter 6), we are bound to exercise a degree of caution before attempting any generalisation because the study was small-scale and highly localised. The need for caution applies *a fortiori* to the study by Maitles and Cowan (1999) on Holocaust education in the primary school. The value of this piece of research lies less in its findings than in its originality, for the sample was minuscule and, as the authors readily concede, not at all representative of Scottish primary school teachers.

The appropriate response to these criticisms is not to dismiss the research on account of its inadequate sampling, but to argue instead for an expanded research base. We need more studies of the kind we have reported, especially if they are undertaken in contrasting geographical settings and include teachers and students from diverse backgrounds. The design of the investigations, in other words, should take cognisance of the possibility that both the way the Holocaust is taught and the learning that results, will vary as a function of a multiplicity of factors including gender, ethnicity and religious affiliation.

While we may be reluctant to generalise the findings from the few studies that are available, we repeat that there is no suggestion that the studies themselves are invalid and thus make no contribution to knowledge. On the contrary, they have to be taken seriously for they reveal, among other things, that some teachers (and *perhaps* a great many) approach the Holocaust in ways that prevent their students from fully coming to terms with it. We are thinking, for example, of those staff who seemed content to devote minimal attention to the subject and those who were overly protective of the sensitivities of their students, refusing to show them film footage they considered too harrowing. Other practices that caused us concern include the apparent willingness of a majority of teachers to make a start on the substantive issues without prior engagement with their students' perceptions of Jews and Judaism and a tendency on the part of a minority, when talking about the Holocaust, to emphasise racism *rather* than anti-Semitism. Such failings risk leaving students with a distorted understanding of the Holocaust and an inability to appreciate its true significance.

To some extent, teachers can be assisted to deal with the Holocaust effectively through continuing professional development, but the number of teachers who can be reached by this means is limited. Moreover, because any such professional development in the foreseeable future would be voluntary in nature, many teachers in need of help may not seek it. In light of these difficulties, it is our contention that a more sensible option would be to tackle the issues surrounding Holocaust education through initial teacher training. Regrettably, we cannot offer any sort of prescription, for there appears to be no research on the kind of provision that is made for students planning to teach the Holocaust as part of the history curriculum in secondary schools. We do not even know whether provision of any kind exists. We certainly know nothing about the attitudes of the trainers themselves towards teaching the subject. Do they acknowledge, for example, that it makes demands on teachers and pupils that are significantly different from those made by other topics their students will be required to teach? And if they do acknowledge these additional demands, do they feel equipped to meet them? On the basis of our own research, we would be particularly keen to discover whether trainee teachers are helped to inform less able pupils about the Holocaust, for it is this section of the student body that is arguably most vulnerable to neo-Nazi propaganda. Of equal concern to us is whether trainees are taught to view the Holocaust simply as history or whether they are encouraged to see it also as a means of exploring the nature of racism. There is clearly much scope for researching the place of teacher training in respect of Holocaust education and we would urge that it be given a high priority.

It should not, however, be seen as the only matter requiring urgent attention. We are conscious of the fact that throughout the book our principal concerns have been discussed in the context of teaching history. Yet we suspect that the Holocaust is taught in many secondary schools as part of the English curriculum (see, for example, McGuinn, 2000) and, in England and Wales, as an integral element of pupils' religious education (Foster and Mercier, 2000). We also know of pressures to expand its role in the teaching of geography (Machon and Lambert, 2001). Such awareness throws up a host of additional questions about how the subject is to be handled. In relation to English we need to ask about the books, poems and plays that are selected and the grounds on which they are deemed to be appropriate. We need to find out whether this literature is studied at the same time as the Holocaust is taught as part of the history curriculum, at an earlier stage or at a later one. And more generally, we should enquire about the sorts of problems teachers face and how they cope with them. Some of the same questions have to be raised in respect of religious education, but crucially, as far as this subject is concerned, we should also determine how, if at all, the Christian origins of anti-Semitism are dealt with and how, from a religious perspective, the Holocaust is to be explained. Indeed, we wonder if students are offered, and allowed to discuss, theological explanations of any kind. [The study by Brown and Davies (1998), referred to in Chapter 5, focused, in part, on religious education, but shed no light on these matters.]

While we are alert to the fact that the Holocaust often features in the teaching of history, English and religious education, we do not know the extent of its treatment elsewhere in the curriculum or anything about the attitudes and practices of staff who may be involved. As far as we are aware, there is no substantial research that looks at how the subject is taught in any discipline other than history. This is a major gap in our knowledge, and one that must be filled, for not only might there be much duplication, and, as a result, much wasting of valuable time; it is also possible that the Holocaust in these other curricular areas is approached in ways that contradict the good practice we have been at pains to elucidate.

Bibliography

Abella, I. and Bialystok, F. (1996) Canada, in: D. S. Wyman (ed.) *The World Reacts to the Holocaust*, Baltimore, The Johns Hopkins University Press.

Adorno, T. W., Frenkel-Brunswick, E., Levinson, D. and Sanford, N. (1950) *The Authoritarian Personality*, New York, Harper.

Alexander, R. J. (1984) *Primary Teaching*, London, Holt, Rinehart and Winston.

Allport, G. W. (1954) *The Nature of Prejudice*, Cambridge, MA, Addison-Wesley.

Améry, J. (1980) *At the Mind's Limits: Contemplations by a Survivor on Auschwitz and Its Realities*, Bloomington, Indiana University Press.

Anne Frank Educational Trust (1996) *Anne Frank*, London, Anne Frank Educational Trust.

Anne Frank Educational Trust (2000) *Anne Frank Declaration: Using the Anne Frank Declaration to Teach About Human Rights, Citizenship and Democracy*, London, Anne Frank Educational Trust.

Arendt, H. (1963) *Eichmann in Jerusalem: A Report on the Banality of Evil*, New York, Viking Press.

Austin, N. (2000) Living to Tell the Tale: Eva's Story, *London Jewish News*, 28 January.

Bardige, B. (1981) Facing History and Ourselves: tracing development through analysis of student journals, *Moral Education, Forum* (Summer).

Barker, M. (1981) *The New Racism*, London, Junction Books.

Baron, S. (1952) *A Social and Religious History of the Jews* 2nd ed., New York, Columbia University Press.

Bartov, O. (1996) Ordinary Monsters, *The New Republic*, 29 April, pp. 32-38.

Bartov, O. (1998) The lessons of the Holocaust, *Dimensions: A Journal of Holocaust Studies*, 12, pp. 13-20.

Bauer, Y. (1978) *The Holocaust in Historical Perspective*, Seattle, University of Washington Press.

Bauer, Y. (1980) *The Jewish Emergence from Powerlessness*, London, Macmillan.

Bauman, Z. (1989) *Modernity and the Holocaust*, Cambridge, Polity Press.

Baumrind, D. (1964) Some thoughts on the ethics of reading Milgram's 'Behavioural Study of Obedience', *American Psychologist*, 19, pp. 421-423.

Belloc, H. (1922) *The Jews*, London, Constable.

Biale, D. (1986) *Power and Powerlessness in Jewish History: The Jewish Tradition and the Myth of Passivity*, New York, Schocken Books.

Bialystok, F. (2000) *Delayed Impact: The Holocaust and the Canadian Jewish Community*, Montreal, McGill-Queen's University Press.

Bonnett, A. and Carrington, B. (1996) Constructions of anti-racist education in Britain and Canada, *Comparative Education*, 32, pp. 271-288.

Brandt, G. (1986) *The Realisation of Antiracist Teaching*, Lewes, Falmer Press.

Brabeck, M., Kenny, M., Stryker, S., Tollefson, T. and Stern Strom, M. (1994) Human Rights Education through the 'Facing History and Ourselves' Program, *Journal of Moral Education*, 23, 3, pp. 333-347.

Braybrooke, M. (1993) Rethinking Christian theology in the shadow of the Shoah, *British Journal of Holocaust Education*, 2, 1, pp. 68-77.

Braybrooke, M. (1998) The Holocaust and British museums: A Christian response, *The Journal of Holocaust Education*, 7, pp. 68-70.

Brecher, B. (1999) Understanding the Holocaust: The uniqueness debate, *Radical Philosophy* (July/August) pp. 17-28.

Brehm, J. W. A. (1966) *A Theory of Psychological Reactance*, New York, Academic Press.

Brook, S. (1989) *The Club: Jews of Modern Britain*, London, Pan Books.

Brown, A. (1999) Beth Shalom Holocaust Memorial Centre, *RE Today* (Spring) pp. 8-9.

Brown, M. and Davies, I. (1998) The Holocaust and Education for Citizenship; the teaching of history, religion and human rights in England, *Educational Review*, 50, 1, pp. 75-83.

Bruchfeld, S. (2000) *Facing Denial in Society and Education*, Paper presented at the Stockholm International Forum on the Holocaust, 26-28 January.

Bruner, J. (1960) *The Process of Education*, New York, Vintage Books.

Butz. A. (1976) *The Hoax of the Twentieth Century*, Richmond, Surrey; Historical Review Press.

Carrington, B. and Short, G. (1989) *'Race' and the Primary School: Theory into Practice*, Windsor, NFER/Nelson.

Carrington, B. and Short, G. (1993) Probing children's prejudice - A consideration of the ethical and methodological issues raised by research and curriculum development, *Educational Studies*, 19, 2, pp. 163-181.

Cesarani, D. (1996) Great Britain, in: D. S. Wyman (ed.) *The World Reacts to the Holocaust*, Baltimore, The Johns Hopkins University Press.

Cesarani, D. (1999) We laughed till we died, *Times Higher Education Supplement*, 28 May.

Cesarani, D. (2000) Seizing the Day: Why Britain will benefit from Holocaust Memorial Day, *Patterns of Prejudice*, 34, 4, pp. 61-66.

Cesarani, D. (2003) Community and disunity, *Jewish Chronicle*, 24 October.

Cheyette, B. (1990) Hilaire Belloc and the 'Marconi Scandal' 1900 - 1914: A re-assessment of the interactionist model of racial hatred, in: T. Kushner and K. Lunn (eds) *The Politics of Marginality: Race, the Radical Right and Minorities in Twentieth Century Britain*, London, Frank Cass.

Clark, K. and Clark, M. (1947) Racial Identification and Preference in Negro Children, in: T. M. Newcombe and E. L. Hartley (eds) *Readings in Social Psychology*, New York, Holt, Rinehart and Winston.

Cohen, P. (1989) *Tracking Common Sense Racism*, London, Cultural Studies Project.

Cole, T. (1999) *Images of the Holocaust: the Myth of the Shoah Business*, London, Gerald Duckworth and Co.

Cornwell, J. (1999) *Hitler's Pope: The Secret History of Pius XII*, Harmondsworth, Viking.

Cornwell, T. (1996) Massacre denied a page in history, *Times Higher Education Supplement*, 12 July.

D'Souza, D. (1995) *The End of Racism*, New York, The Free Press.

Dalrymple, J. (1992) Holocaust lies of the new Nazis, *British Journal of Holocaust Education*, 1, pp. 202-212.

Davey, A. (1983) *Learning to be Prejudiced*, London, Edward Arnold.

Dawidowicz, L. (1992) *What's the Use of Jewish History?*, New York, Schocken Books.

Dei, G. J. S. (1993) The challenges of anti-racist education in Canada, *Canadian Ethnic Studies*, 25, 2, pp. 36-51.

de Laine, M. (1997) Third of teenagers deny Holocaust, *Times Educational Supplement*, 4 July.

Department for Education and Employment (DfEE) (1998) *Education for Citizenship and the Teaching of Democracy in Schools*, London, Qualifications and Curriculum Authority.

Department of Education and Science (1985) *Education for All* Report of the Committee of Enquiry into the Education of Children from Ethnic Minority groups (Swann Report) Cmnd. 9453, London, HMSO.

Department of Education and Science (1989) *National Curriculum: History Working Group Interim Report*, London, HMSO.

Dewey, J. (1916) *Democracy and Education*, New York, Macmillan.

Donaldson, M. (1978) *Children's Minds*, Glasgow, Fontana/Collins.

Downey, M. and Kelly, A. V. (1986) *Theory and Practice of Education* 3rd ed., London, Harper and Row.

Dunn, J. (1988) *The Beginnings of Social Understanding*, Oxford, Blackwell.

Epstein, D. (1993) *Changing Classroom Cultures: Antiracism, Politics and Schools*, Stoke-on-Trent, Trentham Books.

Facing History and Ourselves (1994) *Resource Book - Holocaust and Human Behaviour*, Brookline, MA, Facing History and Ourselves National Foundation.

Faurisson, R. (1979) *The Rumour of Auschwitz*, New York, Revisionist Press.

Fein, H. (1979) *Accounting for Genocide: National Responses and Jewish Victimization During the Holocaust*, London, The Free Press.

Finkelstein, N. (2000) *The Holocaust Industry*, London, Verso.

Fisk, R. (1996) Turning a blind eye to history, *The Independent*, 30 August.

Foster, S. and Mercier, C. (2000) Teaching the Holocaust through Religious Education, in: I. Davies (ed.) *Teaching the Holocaust: Educational Dimensions, Principles and Practice*, London, Continuum.

Frankl, V. (1962) *Man's Search for Meaning*, Boston, MA, Beacon Press.

Gilbert, M. (1986) *The Holocaust: The Jewish Tragedy*, London, Collins.

Gill, L. (2004) How the Holocaust was more than just racism, *The Times (T2)* 21 January.

Gillborn, D. (1995) *Racism and Antiracism in Real Schools*, Buckingham, Open University Press.

Glickman, Y. and Bardikoff, A. (1982) *The Treatment of the Holocaust in Canadian History and Social Science Textbooks*, Toronto, B'Nai B'rith.

Goldberg, M. (1996) Children's autobiographies and diaries of the Holocaust, *Teaching History*, 83, pp. 8-12.

Goldhagen, D. J. (1996) *Hitler's Willing Executioners: Ordinary Germans and the Holocaust*, London, Little Brown.

Gross, J. T. (2001) *Neighbors: The Destruction of the Jewish Community in Jedwabne*, New Jersey, Princeton University Press.

Grugeon, E. and Woods, P. (1990) *Educating All: Multicultural Perspectives in the Primary School*, London, Routledge.

Harney, S. (1996) Anti-racism, Ontario style, *Race and Class*, 37, pp. 35-45.

Harwood, D. (1986) To advocate or educate, *Education 3-13*, 14, pp. 51-57.

Hegel, G. W. (1818) *Lectures on the Philosophy of History*, trans. (1956) J. Sibree (New York, Dover).

Henriques, J. (1984) Social Psychology and the politics of racism, in: J. Henriques, W. Holloway, C. Urwin, C. Venn and V. Walkerdine (eds) *Changing the Subject: Psychology, Social Regulation and Subjectivity*, London, Methuen.

Hertzberg A. (1979) *Being Jewish in America*, New York, Schocken Books.

Hilberg, R. (1985) *The Destruction of the European Jews*, New York, Holmes and Meier.

Hirst, P. and Peters, R. (1970) *The Logic of Education*, London, Routledge and Kegan Paul.

Huerta, C. C. and Shiffman-Huerta, D. (1996) Holocaust Denial Literature: Its Place in Teaching the Holocaust, in: R. Millan (ed.) *New Perspectives on the Holocaust*, New York, New York University Press.

Huyssen, A. (1994) Monument and Memory in a Postmodern Age, in: J. E. Young (ed.) *The Art of Memory: Holocaust Memorials in History*, New York, Prestel.

Iganski, P. and Kosmin, B. (2003) *A New Antisemitism? Debating Judeophobia in 21st-Century Britain*, London, Profile Books.

Janis, I. L. and Feshback, S. (1953) Effects of fear-arousing communications, *Journal of Abnormal and Social Psychology*, 48, 78-92.

Jeansonne, G. (1999) The Right-Wing Mothers of Wartime America, *History Today*, pp. 31-37, December.

Jeffcoate, R. (1984) *Ethnic Minorities and Education*, London, Harper and Row.

Julius, A. (2000) England's Gifts to Jew Hatred, *The Spectator*, 11 November, pp. 12-14.

Karpf, A. (1996) *The War After: Living with the Holocaust*, London, Heinemann.

Katz, S. (1994) *The Holocaust in Historical Context* vol. 1, Oxford, Oxford University Press.

Kelly, K. (1996) Visible Minorities: a diverse group, http://www.statcan.ca/Documents/English/Soc Trends/vismin.html.

King, R. (1978) *All Things Bright and Beautiful? A Sociological Study of Infants' Classrooms*, Chichester, Wiley.

Kirman, J. (1986) James Keegstra and the Eckville High School incident, *The History and Social Science Teacher*, 21, pp. 209-211.

Kochan, L. (1989) Life over Death, *Jewish Chronicle*, 22 December.

Kushner, T. (1989) The British and the Shoah, *Patterns of Prejudice*, 23, pp. 3-17.

Kushner, T. (1994) *The Holocaust and the Liberal Imagination: A Social and Cultural History*, Oxford, Blackwell.

Kushner, T. (1995) Holocaust survivors in Britain: An overview and research agenda, *The Journal of Holocaust Education*, 4, 2, pp. 147-166.

Landau, R. (1989) No Nazi war in British history? *Jewish Chronicle*, 25 August.

Landau, R (1992) *The Nazi Holocaust*, London, I. B. Taurus.

Leigh, A. (1997) Extremists manipulate teaching of history, *Times Educational Supplement*, 4 July.

Levi, P. (1987) *If This is a Man*, London, Abacus.

Levi, T. (1998) Speaking out: The education work of a Holocaust survivor, *The Journal of Holocaust Education* 7, pp. 133-122.

Lewis, B. (1987) *Semites and Antisemites*, New York, W. W. Norton and Co.

Lewy, G. (1999) Gypsies and Jews under the Nazis, *Holocaust and Genocide Studies*, 13, 3, pp. 383-404.

Lipstadt, D. (1992) Holocaust-denial and the compelling force of reason, *Patterns of Prejudice*, 26, 1/2 pp. 64-76.

Lipstadt, D. (1993) *Denying the Holocaust: the Growing Assault on Truth and Memory*, New York, The Free Press.

Lipstadt, D. E. (1995) Not facing history, *The New Republic*, 6 March, pp. 26-29.

Lorenz, D. (1996) Anti-Semitism in the tradition of German discourse: The path to the Holocaust, in: R. L. Millen (ed.) *New Perspectives on the Holocaust*, New York, New York University Press.

Lynch, J. (1987) *Prejudice Reduction and the Schools*, London, Cassell Educational Limited.

Machon, P. and Lambert, D. (2001) Citizenship denied: the case of the Holocaust, in: D. Lambert and P. Machon (eds) *Citizenship Through Geography Education*, London, Routledge/Falmer.

Macpherson, W. (1999) *The Stephen Lawrence Inquiry*, London, The Stationery Office Ltd.

Maitles, H. and Cowan, P. (1999) Teaching the Holocaust in primary schools in Scotland: modes, methodology and content, *Educational Review*, 51, 3, pp. 263-272.

Marrus, M. (1995) Getting it right: A historian thinking of the Holocaust, in: J. F. Grafstein (ed.) *Beyond Imagination: Canadians Write about the Holocaust*, Toronto, McClelland and Stewart.

Matar, J. (2001) In Denial, *The Jerusalem Report*, 23 April, pp. 26-27.

McGuinn, N. (2000) Teaching the Holocaust through English, in: I. Davies (ed.) *Teaching the Holocaust: Educational Dimensions, Principles and Practice*, London, Continuum.

McGuire, W. J. (1969) The nature of attitudes and attitude change, in: G. Lindzey and A. Aronson (eds) *Handbook of Social Psychology* vol. 3, 2nd ed., Reading, MA, Addison-Wesley.

Milgram, S. (1974) *Obedience to Authority: An Experimental View*, New York, Harper and Row.

Milner, D. (1983) *Children and Race: Ten Years On*, London, Ward Lock Educational.

Mock, K. (2000) Holocaust and hope: Holocaust education in the context of anti-racist education in Canada, in: F. C. De Coste and B. Schwartz (eds) *The Holocaust's Ghost: Writings on Art, Politics, Law and Education*, Edmonton, University of Alberta Press.

Modood, T. (1989) Religious anger and minority rights, *Political Quarterly*, 60, 3, pp. 280-284.

Modood, T. (1992) *Not Easy being British: Colour, Culture and Citizenship*, Stoke-on-Trent, Runnymede Trust and Trentham Books.

Mullard, C. (1980) *Racism in Society and School: History, Policy and Practice*, London, Centre for Multicultural Education.

Nathan, J. (2003) Rebels and a Cause, *Jewish Chronicle*, 17 October.

Niewyk, D. L. (1981) *The Jews in Weimar Germany*, Manchester, Manchester University Press.

Novick, P. (1999) *The Holocaust in American Life*, New York, Houghton Mifflin Co.

Oliner, P. (1986) Legitimating and implementing prosocial education, *Humboldt Journal of Social Relations*, 13, pp. 389-408.

Oliner, S. and Oliner, P. (1988) *The Altruistic Personality: Rescuers of Jews in Nazi Europe*, New York, The Free Press.

Osler, A. (1999) Citizenship, democracy and political literacy, *Multicultural Teaching*, 18, 1, pp. 12-15.

Peters, R. S. (1966) *Ethics and Education*, London, George Allen and Unwin Ltd.

Phillips, M. (1996) *All Must Have Prizes*, London, Little Brown and Co.

Piaget, J. (1932) *The Moral Judgment of the Child*, London, Routledge and Kegan Paul.

Reed, C. A. (1994) The omission of anti-Semitism in anti-racism, *Canadian Women's Studies*, 14, 2, pp. 68-71.

Reed, C. A. and Novogrodsky, M. (2000) Teaching the Holocaust in a multiracial, multicultural, urban environment, in Canada, in: F. C. De Coste and B. Schwartz (eds) *The Holocaust's Ghost: Writings on Art, Politics, Law and Education*, Edmonton, University of Alberta Press.

Reitlinger, G. (1953) *The Final Solution*, New York, A. S. Barnes.

Rendell, F. (1987) *Into Hiding: A Topic Study on Anne Frank*, Glasgow, University of Strathclyde.

Richter, H. P. (1987) *Friedrich*, New York, Puffin Books.

Rittner, C., Smith, S. D. and Steinfeldt, I. (eds) (2000) *The Holocaust and the Christian World*, London, Kuperard.

Rosenberg, A. (1934) *The Myth of the Twentieth Century: An Evaluation of the Spiritual-Intellectual Confrontations of Our Age*, Munich, Hoheneichen-Verlag.

Ross, A. (1984) Developing political concepts and skills in the primary school, *Educational Review*, 36, 2, pp. 131-139.

Rubinstein, P. and Taylor, W. (1992) Teaching about the Holocaust in the National Curriculum, *The British Journal of Holocaust Education*, 1, pp. 47-54.

Rubinstein, W. D. (1997) *The Myth of Rescue*, London, Routledge.

Runnymede Trust (1994) *A Very Light Sleeper: The Persistence and Danger of Antisemistism*, London, Runnymede Trust.

Santayana, G. (1905) *The Life of Reason*, vol. 1, New York, Charles Scribner's Sons.

Schwimmer, W. (2000) Message delivered by the Secretary General of the Council of Europe at the Stockholm International Forum on the Holocaust, 26-28 January.

Sepinwall, H. (1999) Incorporating Holocaust education into K-4 curriculum and teaching in the United States, *Social Studies and the Young Learner*, 10, pp. 5-8.

Sewell, B. (1999) Manchester's big mistake, *Evening Standard*, 27 April.

Shawn, K. (1999) What should they read, and when should they read it? A selective review of Holocaust literature for students in grades 2 through 6, in: J. P. Robertson (ed.) *Teaching for a Tolerant World*, Urbana, Illinois: National Council of Teachers of English.

Shoemaker, R. (2003) Teaching the Holocaust in America's Schools: some considerations for teachers, *Intercultural Education*, 14, 2, 191-200.

Short, G. (1991a) Teaching the Holocaust: Some reflections on a problematic area, *British Journal of Religious Education*, 14, 1, pp. 28-34.

Short, G. (1991b) Combatting anti-Semitism: A dilemma for antiracist education, *British Journal of Educational Studies*, 39, 1, pp. 33-44.

Short, G. (1994a) Teaching the Holocaust: the relevance of children's perceptions of Jewish culture and identity, *British Educational Research Journal*, 20, pp. 393-406.

Short, G. (1994b) Teaching about the Holocaust: A consideration of some ethical and pedagogic issues, *Educational Studies*, 20, 1, pp. 53-68.

Short, G. (1995) The Holocaust in the National Curriculum: A survey of teachers' attitudes and practices, *Journal of Holocaust Education*, 4, pp. 167-188.

Short, G. (1999) Teaching the Holocaust in Toronto: A response to Lucy Dawidowicz, *Canadian and International Education*, 28, 1, pp. 17-36.

Short, G. (2000a) The Holocaust Museum as an Educational Resource: A View from New York City, *The Journal of Holocaust Education* 9, 3, pp. 1-18.

Short, G. (2000b) Holocaust education in Ontario high schools: An antidote to racism? *Cambridge Journal of Education*, 30, 2, pp. 291-306.

Short, G. and Carrington, B. (1991) Unfair discrimination: Teaching the principles to children of primary school age, *Journal of Moral Education*, 20, 2, pp. 157-177.

Short, G. and Carrington, B. (1995) Learning about Judaism: A contribution to the debate on multifaith religious education, *British Journal of Religious Education* 17, 3, pp. 157-167.

Singh, B. (1988) The teaching of controversial issues: the problems of the neutral-chair approach, in: B. Carrington and B. Troyna (eds) *Children and Controversial Issues: Strategies for the Early and Middle Years of Schooling*, Lewes, Falmer Press.

Siraj-Blatchford, I. (1994) *Early Years: Laying the Foundations for Racial Equality*, Stoke-on-Trent, Trentham Books.

Skvirsky, M. (2000) Facing History and Ourselves: News (Spring) pp. 4-5.

Smith, S. D. (1999) *Making Memory: Creating Britain's First Holocaust Centre*, Newark, Quill Press.

Stenhouse, L. (1975) *The Humanities Curriculum Project: An Introduction*, London, Heinemann.

Stone, D. (2000) Day of Remembrance or Day of Forgetting? Or, why Britain does not need a Holocaust Memorial Day, *Patterns of Prejudice*, 34, 4, pp. 53-59.

Stradling, R., Noctor, M. and Bains, B. (1984) *Teaching Controversial Issues*, London, Edward Arnold.

Supple, C. (1992) The Teaching of the Nazi Holocaust in North Tyneside, Newcastle and Northumberland Secondary Schools, Unpublished manuscript, School of Education, University of Newcastle-upon-Tyne.

Supple, C. (1993a) The teaching of the Holocaust, *AJEX Journal* 16, p. 21.

Supple, C. (1993b) *From Prejudice to Genocide: Learning about the Holocaust*, Stoke-on-Trent, Trentham Books.

Totten, S. (1999) Should there be Holocaust education for K-4 students? The answer is no, *Social Studies and the Young Learner*, September/October, 12, pp. 36-39.

Troper, H. (1991) Canada's Multiculturalism:Policy and Reality, Paper presented at A World of Difference Conference, Case Western University, Cleveland, Ohio.

Troyna, B. (1993) *Racism and Education*, Buckingham, Open University Press.

Troyna, B. and Carrington, B. (1990) *Education, Racism and Reform*, London, Routledge.

Troyna, B. and Williams, J. (1986) *Racism, Education and the State*, Beckenham, Croom Helm.

Vygotsky, L. (1956) *Selected Psychological Research*, Moscow, Academy of Pedagogic Sciences.

Wells, M. and Wingate, J. (1985) Holocaust studies as anti-racist education, *The History and Social Science Teacher*, 20, pp. 205-208.

Wheatcroft, G. (1996) *The Controversy of Zion*, London, Sinclair-Stevenson.

Wiesel, E. (1960) *Night*, New York, Avon Books.

Wiesel, E. (1983) Does the Holocaust lie beyond the reach of art? *New York Times*, 17 April.

Willis, P. (1977) *Learning to Labour*, Farnborough, Saxon House.

Wistrich, R. (1999) Is anti-Semitism dead or just sleeping? *Jewish Chronicle*, November 12.

Wood, D. (1998) *How Children Learn and Think*, Oxford, Blackwell.

Wyman, D. S. (1996a) The United States, in: D. S. Wyman (ed.) *The World Reacts to the Holocaust*, Baltimore, The Johns Hopkins University Press.

Wyman, D. S. (1996b) (ed.) *The World Reacts to the Holocaust*, Baltimore, The Johns Hopkins University Press.

Young, J. E. (1999) America's Holocaust: Memory and the Politics of Identity, in: H. Flanzbaum (ed.) *The Americanization of the Holocaust*, Baltimore, The Johns Hopkins University Press.

Zimbardo, P. (1972) The Pathology of Imprisonment, *Societies*, April, p. 109.

Name Index

Subject Index